BACKYARD BIRDFEEDING FOR BEGINNERS

BACKYARD BIRDFEEDING

FOR

BEGINNERS

MATHEW TEKULSKY

ILLUSTRATIONS BY
JOHN BURGOYNE

Gramercy Books / New York

This 2003 edition published by Gramercy Books, an imprint of Random House Value Publishing, a division of Random House, Inc., New York, by arrangement with the author.

Gramercy Books is a registered trademark and the colophon is a trademark of Random House, Inc.

Printed in the United States of America.

Random House
New York • Toronto • London • Sydney • Auckland
www.randomhouse.com

Library of Congress Cataloging-in-Publication Data

Tekulsky, Mathew, 1954-
Backyard birdfeeding for beginners / Mathew Tekulsky ; illustrations by John Burgoyne.
p. cm.
Originally published: New York : Three Rivers Press, c1999.
ISBN 0-517-22150-0
1. Birds—Feeding and feeds. 2. Bird feeders. 3. Birdhouses. 4. Bird attracting. 5. Birds.
I. Burgoyne, John. II. Title.

QL676.5 .T38 2002
598'.07'234—dc21
2002029744

9 8 7 6 5 4 3 2 1

To my mother

CONTENTS

Contents

Contents

CHAPTER SEVEN:

TWENTY COMMON GARDEN BIRDS   129

Contents

A C K N O W L E D G M E N T S

AT CROWN PUBLISHERS, I would like to thank Steve Magnuson for his great book idea, Brandt Aymar for offering me this project, and PJ Dempsey for shepherding the book through to production. I would also like to thank my literary agent, Jane Jordan Browne, for her continued support and encouragement.

INTRODUCTION

YOU ARE SITTING in the middle of your backyard bird garden. A bright blue Scrub Jay plucks an unshelled, raw peanut from your platform feeder, while a group of about ten male and female House Finches pick the black oil sunflower seeds out from the mixed birdseed you have spread out for them on the grass. (You can hear the faint cracking of the shells in their mouths, and it sounds like a symphony.)

Your male Anna's Hummingbird spots an Allen's Hummingbird taking nectar from a star clusters bush and promptly chases the interloper over the tall oleander border and off the property, appearing moments later at his perch on a spike of yucca. He *whzzes* in triumph, then makes a beeline for the sugar water in the hummingbird feeder that hangs from a branch of your apricot tree.

As the midafternoon sun blazes down between the branches and leaves of your lemon tree, where you have hung an oriole feeder, the male Hooded Oriole flutters in to his perch, *chucking* along the way to make sure all competitors give him a wide berth. As he takes short sips of the sugar water in the feeder, you marvel at how his bright yellow feathers juxtapose against his black chin, neck, wings, and tail. Moments later, his pale yellow mate flies in to the lemon tree and picks her way over to the feeder, taking short sips like the male. Then they both fly off into the canyon. Up from Mexico, they are a taste of the tropics, only here during the spring and summer.

And so it is in your backyard bird garden, as the days slowly slip by.

Occasionally, a group of Bushtits flitters through the oleander, the lemon tree, and off into the canyon.

A Red-tailed Hawk circles high overhead almost every day, catching the warm thermals and perching on a palm tree on the hill above your house.

The Northern Mockingbirds scatter about, calling out with their mellifluous song, though they rarely feed in the yard. (You have been meaning to start a compost pile that will provide insects for them, but you have not gotten around to it yet.)

But how did all of this come to pass? A couple of months ago, the only birds seen in the yard were the occasional finches eating seeds from the tall grass, or a hummingbird nectaring on the Mexican sage and lavender.

Now, the yard is awash with birds, all demonstrating their unique feeding habits, calls, schedules, and distinct behavior.

You know the birds by now, but operating your bird garden was not this routine at the beginning.

In this book, you will learn how to start your own backyard bird garden, from the ground up.

The birds in your garden may be different from the birds that are featured here, but the basic principles of how to attract a wide variety of birds to your garden are universal.

Provide the birds with the food, water, shelter, and nesting sites that they need, and the birds will descend upon your yard as if it were a magnet.

Then you will be living with your birds, and you will wonder how it could ever have been otherwise.

My backyard bird garden, in the Brentwood Hills section of Los Angeles, has been a labor of love for me for years. As the culmination of my fascination with all forms of nature, which began with me as a child, my garden gives me the opportunity to witness many species of birds in all their glory, daily.

Throughout the seasons, I observe the arrivals and departures of migrating birds such as the Hooded Oriole; the nest-building activities of my resident Northern Mockingbirds; the constant antics of the family of Scrub Jays that live in my neighborhood and spend as much time in my yard as I do; and the wonderful buzzing of the hummingbirds as they weave their way throughout my garden.

All of these experiences connect me with the rhythms

of the natural world, and if you start a backyard bird garden of your own, you, too, will enjoy all of the benefits of having the birds around you.

So let us get started!

BACKYARD
BIRDFEEDING
FOR
BEGINNERS

Getting Started

BIRD HISTORY AND RANGES

EVER SINCE *ARCHAEOPTERYX* appeared on Earth about 150 million years ago, birds have been evolving into the species that we see in our gardens today. Most of today's bird families had evolved by 2 million years ago, and between then and now, most of our modern bird species evolved.

There are more than 9,000 species of birds worldwide. About 800 are in the continental United States and Canada, and about 150 of these are relatively common garden birds. Depending on where you live, forty to fifty of *these* species may appear in your yard, although it is possible to attract many more species that are specific to particular localities.

While the Cedar Waxwing, Dark-eyed Junco, American Goldfinch, and Pine Siskin are common throughout the United States, the Tufted Titmouse, Eastern Bluebird, Northern Cardinal, and Indigo Bunting occur in the East, while the Black Phoebe, Steller's Jay, Western Tanager, and Black-headed Grosbeak occur in the West.

Over the seasons, birds reside either in their summer (or breeding) range or in their winter range. By learning when during the year each species of bird will be in your area, and for how long, you can best be prepared to provide the food, water, shelter, and (perhaps) nesting sites that they might need.

Whichever birds you have gracing your garden, they will become special to you. We may not all be lucky enough to have such spectacularly colorful species as the Northern Cardinal or the Indigo Bunting in our yards, but every bird is unique and has its own beauty, physically and otherwise—just like all people.

So rejoice in the presence of the birds in your yard and enjoy them for who and what they are.

BIRD BIOLOGY

All birds are warm-blooded, and all of them have feathers—although not all can fly. All birds lay eggs, and most build a nest out of twigs, plant fibers, and other matter (both natural and otherwise) in which to raise the brood or two (sometimes three) that they have each season.

Most birds incubate their eggs for about two weeks, and the young usually remain in the nest for two to three weeks until they fledge, or fly off on their own. In some cases, as with the American Goldfinch, adult birds continue to feed their fledglings for up to a month after they leave the nest; in others, as with the Mallard, the young become independent almost as soon as they hatch.

Birds have remarkable powers of sight. In almost all species, the eyes are placed on the sides of the head, resulting in monocular vision. That is, they see a different scene on each side of their head and only have overlapping (or binocular) sight when they look directly forward. For this reason, you may see the birds in your garden bobbing their heads from time to time, to get a better look at you. Owls, of course, have binocular vision as humans do, but see much better at night than we can.

Birds also have incredible powers of flight—each species in its own way. While the Ruby-throated Hummingbird migrates across the Gulf of Mexico to its wintering grounds in Mexico and Central America each year, the Scarlet Tanager follows a similar route but continues on to northwestern South

America. Meanwhile, each winter, American Robins that breed in the northern latitudes of North America join their brethren who are residents in the southern latitudes.

And so, each species of bird in its own way manages to fill its niche in nature.

BIRD BILLS

You can tell what a bird likes to eat by looking at his bill.

Large, nutcracker-like bills, such as those of the Northern Cardinal and Evening Grosbeak, are perfectly designed for eating larger seeds. Other seed-eaters, such as the House Finch, Song Sparrow, Dark-eyed Junco, Pine Siskin, Indigo Bunting, and American Goldfinch, have smaller bills than these former two, but can still manage to crack open most seeds.

By contrast, birds such as the Yellow Warbler, House Wren, Wood Thrush, American Robin, and

Red-eyed Vireo have slender bills that are perfect for snagging insects out of the ground or from tree trunks. Indeed, the Brown Creeper even has a curved bill that is expressly designed for this purpose; and the Red Crossbill has crossed mandibles that allow it to extract pine nuts from the cones of pine trees, as well as the seeds of other conifers.

The Hooded Oriole, on the other hand, has a long, curved bill that is designed for extracting nectar from flowers—or from oriole feeders. And the Downy Woodpecker has a bill that acts as a chisel, allowing it to burrow into tree trunks and extract a wide variety of insects—as well as enabling it to carve out a cavity in the wood in which to nest.

BIRDCALLS

Likewise, each species of bird has its own distinctive call, or variety of calls, with which you will become familiar in your own garden.

My delightful Scrub Jay has a short, upwardly rising screech sound that he uses when perched in the palm tree overlooking the side yard that serves as my backyard bird garden.

This screech sound has a number of meanings.

First and foremost, it serves as an identifying call to his mate, letting her know his presence.

However, if I walk out of the house and the Scrub

Jay sees me (and the platform feeder has no unshelled peanuts on it), he will give me one of his screeches and will repeat it a few moments later if I take no action.

Feeling guilty, I retreat into the house and put a handful of peanuts on the platform feeder.

Now the Scrub Jay flies down to retrieve the peanuts, but after clutching the first one in his bill and flying to a nearby perch, he lets out his characteristic screech sound.

Moments later, his mate flies into the flowering plum and then descends onto the platform feeder, plucking her own peanut from on top of the mixed birdseed.

So the screech sound means "Here I am" as well as "There is food here."

But the Scrub Jay is not finished there.

If he arrives back earlier than his mate and she suddenly shows up, he may give her a low, gurgling, guttural call that sounds like a Geiger counter, as if he is saying, "I have first dibs on the next peanut—back off."

Sure enough, his mate waits until he takes the next peanut, and then she flies down to take her next one—always flying off either to store it somewhere in the garden or beyond, or to eat it somewhere out of sight, where there is time and (presumably) safety to peck open the shell and eat the nut.

The Scrub Jay has yet another call, a high-pitched *screech, screech, screech, screech* call, that he uses when aggressively chasing other Scrub Jays (including his mate and their fledglings) out of the side yard and into the canyon. Usually after hearing this sound, I look over just in time to see one jay flying between the yucca and the lemon tree, followed closely by my Scrub Jay. Then they both dive down the hill, disappearing from sight and traveling at about thirty miles per hour.

So by becoming familiar with the calls of your birds, you can get quite an insight into their character and behavior.

OBSERVING BIRDS

To best appreciate the colorful display of the birds in your garden, a good pair of binoculars with which to view them is essential.

While looking through my 8×35 binoculars, I have been startled by the shiny blue back and wings of the Scrub Jays; the blazing yellow feathers of the male Hooded Oriole; the rose-red crown and gorget of the male Anna's Hummingbird when the sun catches these colors at just the right angle; the majestic red head and breast of the male House Finch, which looks as if it has been painted on; and the juxtaposition of the Rufous-sided Towhee's jet-black head and neck with the bird's bright rufous sides and white belly.

Looking through binoculars will also enable you to better enter the intimate world of birds that the naked eye does not reveal.

For instance, it may look as if the House Finch is simply chomping down on an unshelled sunflower seed; but did you know that the House Finch, by using its tongue and beak together, turns each sunflower seed in a circle, biting the edges until the shell splits, falls away, and the bird is left with the seed in its mouth?

And have you ever seen anything quite as delicate and charming as a close-up view of the Scrub Jay burying his beak repeatedly into his white breast feathers in a preening session so that his head seems to disappear, then fluffing up these feathers so that he looks like a puffball for a few moments, and then shaking them out and returning to his original position?

And the binoculars revealed, in late July, a Scrub Jay fledgling flying over to another Scrub Jay fledgling on the trunk of the yucca and transferring a dark, grape-sized berry from his mouth to his sibling's, and then the sibling flying off. Later that day, a Scrub Jay fledgling pecked open a black oil sunflower seed on

the platform feeder, and as soon as a tiny piece of the kernel dropped to the platform, out of nowhere another Scrub Jay fledgling appeared, grabbed the tiny seed with his bill, and flew off into the canyon, leaving the original fledgling dumbfounded.

Indeed, if you take anywhere near an active interest in your birds, you will find yourself involuntarily reaching for your binoculars half of the time you are observing your birds' features and behavior in your garden.

This will greatly aid in identifying your birds, but will also help you immeasurably to become as close as you can to witnessing and (hopefully) understanding their behavior, without having to follow them out over hill and dale.

PHOTOGRAPHING BIRDS

Another piece of equipment that is virtually indispensable in your bird garden is a good camera, preferably one with a zoom lens or a powerful tele-photo lens. In my case, I use an 80–210mm zoom lens that is attached to my trusty Honeywell Pentax camera body. Everything is manual, so I can control all aspects of my photography—except the birds themselves, of course.

The zoom lens allows me to get close-up pho-tographs of the birds in my garden, while still giving me the flexibility of zooming in and out of the shot at will in order to obtain the best composition pos-sible for each photo.

Bird photography is a valuable tool for identify-ing the birds in your garden so you can better deter-mine which types of plantings, feeders, and foods to provide for them.

It is also a tremendously challenging creative exercise that will surprise you both with its frustra-tions and with its ultimate rewards.

FIELD GUIDES AND NOTEBOOKS

Finally, you should arm yourself with a national, regional, and perhaps even local field guide for birds, as well as a good notebook in which to record your field notes about the birds in your garden.

Just when you least expect it, a bird species that

you have never before seen will undoubtedly fly into your garden, and you will find yourself scrambling for your binoculars to get a close-up view of it; your field guide to try to identify it; and your notebook to record fresh observations about its physical characteristics and behavior. Of course, the sooner you can get a good photograph of your visitor the better— but a newcomer can easily be flushed at first, especially if he is not familiar with you, or any other humans for that matter.

For my "notebook," I use gummed pads of 8½-by-11-inch, wide-ruled, white paper. I date and number each page consecutively (e.g., 7/4-1), and thereby I have a record of all the birds I have observed in the garden, along with such pertinent facts as when they arrived (or rather, when I first saw them); which natural and human-provided foods they prefer; and any interesting behavior that I have noticed. It is also advisable to record the time of day and weather conditions of your observations, as birds are creatures of habit not only from season to season, but from hour to hour, minute to minute, and second to second.

In this way, you will have a living record of the life of your garden, which will help you to plan from season to season, or simply to reminisce with joy about your experiences over the years with your birds.

RECOMMENDED FIELD GUIDES:

National Geographic Society. *Field Guide to the Birds of North America*. 2d ed. Washington, D.C.: National Geographic Society, 1987.

Peterson, Roger Tory. *A Field Guide to the Birds*. 4th ed. Boston: Houghton Mifflin Co., 1980.

Peterson, Roger Tory. *A Field Guide to Western Birds*. 3d ed. Boston: Houghton Mifflin Co., 1990.

OTHER BIRD-WATCHING ACTIVITIES

Perhaps the most popular activity for backyard bird-watchers is identifying the birds. This is quite a rewarding pastime and can lead to many great discoveries.

The most important things to look for when identifying a bird are its size, its shape (especially its bill), and its coloring and other special markings.

A small bird such as a Lesser Goldfinch (4½″) appears quite a bit smaller than a Dark-eyed Junco (6¼″), which itself appears small in comparison to an American Robin (10″), which is dwarfed by a Pileated Woodpecker (16½″)!

When it comes to shape, nuthatches have short tails while wrens have upturned tails; the Plain Titmouse and Northern Cardinal have crests, while the Black-capped Chickadee and Brown-headed Cowbird do not; and warblers have short, thin bills, while the Brown Thrasher has a long, downturned bill.

Color, of course, is king when it comes to identifying birds, and in this respect, it would be extremely difficult to mistake a bright blue Indigo Bunting with an equally bright orange Northern Oriole or a stunningly red Scarlet Tanager.

In addition, more detailed observation will reveal that a Song Sparrow has a central spot on its breast, whereas the White-crowned and Golden-crowned Sparrows sport headdresses that are indeed white and yellow respectively while the rest of their bodies are strikingly similar.

The Northern Mockingbird's white wing patches, which are visible when it flies, help to identify this mostly gray bird.

Perhaps the most important and valuable reason for identifying the birds in your garden (and beyond) is so that you can develop a list of the species that appear in your area at different times of the year.

If you share this information with your local Audubon Society chapter or another ornithological organization, the body of knowledge regarding your birds and those of your neighbors will be enhanced so that biologists can study the overall populations of birds and adopt methods of conserving them.

You may even want to write an article about your birds for a birding magazine, or perhaps share your findings with other birders all over the world in a chat room on the World Wide Web. There are plenty of birding Web sites, and more are being added all the time as the popularity of the Internet increases.

If you have artistic inclinations, you might want to try your hand at drawing or painting the birds in your yard. Since I'm a terrible drawer, I choose to "paint" my birds with my camera. However, if you *can* draw, sketching the birds in your yard will not only bring you closer to your feathered friends and heighten your awareness of their physical attributes—but it might result in a work of art that you can frame and hang on your wall.

BIRDFEEDING THROUGHOUT THE SEASONS

In many ways, backyard birdfeeding is a yearlong event.

In the winter, birds flock together to forage on whatever seeds, nuts, and other natural food is available. At this time of scarcity, it is tremendously helpful of bird gardeners to supply a few extras for the birds—especially fat- and protein-rich sources of food such as nuts, sunflower seeds, and suet.

In the spring, before the previous season's nuts and seeds appear from under the melting snow, bird gardeners can help sustain both overwintering birds and early-spring migrants by providing a good combination of foods for them. Sometimes, a midspring frost or snowstorm will temporarily diminish the birds' natural food sources, and at these times you can certainly save many birds' lives by giving them the seeds, nuts, and fruits that they need, along with an oasis in which to ride out the storm.

In the summer, when birds are mating and nesting, far more food sources are available (such as flower seeds, insects, and berries), and they generally spread out their territories to accomplish their reproductive goals. However, because their energy needs in feeding themselves and rearing their young are so high, backyard bird gardeners can help the new generations along by providing supplemental foods in the form of seeds, fruits, and berries—as well as nectar for hummingbirds and orioles.

In the fall, just when the migrants need the most energy to sustain themselves on their long flights to the south, the berries and insects that had been so plentiful during the summer gradually begin to disappear as the days become shorter and foraging times diminish. During this stressful part of the year, bird gardeners can help the birds on their way—and maybe even entice a few fall migrants to stick around the yard for the winter.

Each part of the bird-gardening season has its own delights and responsibilities.

Be sure to put your bird feeders out early in the fall. By attracting the resident birds to your garden first, you will gain the attention of migrants, who will drop down out of the skies to see what all the fuss is about.

During the winter, you can gradually move your feeders closer to the house, so that you can sit inside where it is warm and watch your birds feasting at close quarters.

Spring, of course, provides the opportunity to observe the mating rituals of your birds and to hear the males singing out from their territories to attract females. You may not know it yet, but at this time of the year, you have just opened up a bird nursery that will soon be populated with young charges that are ready to take on the world for the first time.

And sure enough, as summer arrives and you see an assortment of fledglings enter your yard in trepidation, you become perhaps as fulfilled as their parents are as they shepherd these juveniles through their first rites of passage—and survival.

Thus, you should treat your backyard bird garden as a living, breathing organism with its own special ebbs and flows throughout the year. In this way, you will provide the best habitat for the birds, and they will respond the most positively toward you.

BIRD CONSERVATION

Central to the art of backyard birdfeeding (and it *is* an art!) is the notion of bird conservation—for not only are you gardening for birds because it pleases and entertains you, you are also playing a pivotal role in preserving and in many cases expanding the functioning habitats for countless birds throughout North America and beyond.

In recent years, as more and more of wild America has been converted into suburbs—and more and more of urban America has been paved over—countless bird gardeners have stepped into the fray to provide the food, water, shelter, and nesting areas that our migratory and resident birds need to survive.

Over the eons, birds and plants have developed a symbiotic relationship, so that the plants provide colorful fruits and berries for the birds to eat, while the birds reciprocate by dispersing all over the countryside the precious seeds that lie within these fruits.

Thus, a savvy bird gardener will plant native trees and shrubs such as dogwood, holly, cherry, hawthorn, juniper, serviceberry, and bayberry, then watch the fruits from these native plants disappear with the birds, only to reappear as seedlings when our hearty bird gardener takes his or her walks around the countryside over the years.

In this way, bird gardeners add to the native plant populations in their surrounding area, as well as on their own properties. When carried out on a national level, the result of such a practice is significant for populations of native plants and birds alike.

Meanwhile, the increasingly popular pastime of providing birdseed at ground, platform, hopper, and tube feeders has resulted in the growth of the populations of many bird species as well as the expansion of their ranges. This is certainly the case with the Tufted Titmouse, Northern Cardinal, Evening Grosbeak, Mourning Dove, and House Finch. Likewise, by providing nectar for the Anna's Hummingbird, this tiny creature's population and range has expanded dramatically, thanks to Western bird gardeners.

Three more tangible ways to become involved with bird conservation are to take part in the National Audubon Society's Christmas Bird Count, as well as in Project FeederWatch and the Great Backyard Bird Count, which are jointly conducted by the Audubon Society and the Cornell Laboratory of Ornithology.

The first Christmas Bird Count was conducted on

Christmas Day in 1900 and consisted of twenty-seven counters conducting twenty-five separate counts, from Toronto, Ontario, to Pacific Grove, California. Today, more than forty-five thousand bird-watchers tally their results in more than seventeen hundred separate counts throughout North America and Latin America as well.

The counts take place from mid-December to early January, and the tabulations from these hearty volunteers have enabled ornithologists to assess the changing populations of many species of birds and their habitats over the last hundred years.

To become involved with the next Christmas Bird Count, contact your local Audubon Society chapter or the National Audubon Society (700 Broadway, New York, NY 10003).

In Project FeederWatch, tabulations are taken at birdfeeders throughout North America from November through March. The program began in 1987 and includes more than thirteen thousand participants, who have amassed a tremendous amount of data involving bird populations and their movements. For instance, Project FeederWatch helped discover that House Finches are expanding their range eastward, while the Carolina Wren has been expanding its range northward. Statistics such as these give us hints about climatic changes and the effect of urban development on our bird populations. In this way, they give us a guide (or a warning?) about our own environmental status.

To become involved with Project FeederWatch, contact the Cornell Laboratory of Ornithology (159 Sapsucker Woods Road, Ithaca, NY 14850).

Nineteen ninety-eight marked the inaugural year of the Great Backyard Bird Count, an on-line bird census conducted February 20–22 through Bird-Source, an on-line bird-research database developed and maintained by the Cornell Laboratory of Ornithology and the National Audubon Society.

Using the one hundred most common backyard birds as compiled by Project FeederWatch, the Great '98 Backyard Bird Count attracted more than fourteen thousand bird-watchers across North America, who reported that the most sightings were of the Mourning Dove, Black-capped Chickadee, Northern Cardinal, Blue Jay, American Crow, Downy Woodpecker, House Finch, Tufted Titmouse, Dark-eyed Junco, and American Goldfinch.

I sent in the following report from my yard on February 20: Mourning Dove (10), Anna's Hummingbird (2), Scrub Jay (4), American Crow (2), Plain Titmouse (2), Bushtit (10), Northern Mockingbird (2), California Thrasher (1), Rufous-sided Towhee (4), California Towhee (4), Song

Sparrow (1), Golden-crowned Sparrow (4), White-crowned Sparrow (4), Dark-eyed Junco (4), and House Finch (10).

I then clicked over from the bird-count form to the Great '98 Count species distribution maps and could see where else in the country people had reported the same species that I had. Thus, I discovered that while the Anna's Hummingbird, Scrub Jay, Bushtit, California Thrasher, California Towhee, and Golden-crowned Sparrow occurred primarily along the West Coast, the Mourning Dove, American Crow, Plain Titmouse, Northern Mockingbird, Rufous-sided Towhee, Song Sparrow, White-crowned Sparrow, Dark-eyed Junco, and House Finch occurred across a wide area of North America.

If you want to become involved with the Great Backyard Bird Count, visit the BirdSource home page on the Internet (http://birdsource.cornell.edu).

TEACHING OUR CHILDREN

Perhaps the best way to promote the conservation of birds, and bird-watching in general, is to get our kids started early in their appreciation and love for nature as a whole, and our marvelous feathered creatures in particular.

There is nothing like seeing the joy in a child's eyes when he or she witnesses his or her first "blue birdie," then gets to know that "birdie" over time.

By introducing our children to the wonders of nature, and by involving them in activities such as setting up a bird garden, learning to identify birds, or perhaps joining a bird club and taking bird-watching field trips, we will be planting the seeds for future conservationists who will then pass on these values to their own children.

And to think that it all started in your very own backyard!

GET READY, GET SET . . .

So now it is time to start building your backyard bird garden.

In the following chapters, you will learn which types of birdfeeders you can use; the various types of food that you can put out for your birds; the different plants that birds use for food, shelter, and nesting; how to provide water for your birds; and some tips on birdhouses.

Enjoy!

C H A P T E R

T W O

Birdfeeders

BIRDS WILL USE MANY types of feeders in your yard. The most popular are the ground feeder, the hopper feeder, the tube feeder, the platform feeder, the window feeder, the suet feeder, and of course, the hummingbird and oriole feeders.

GROUND FEEDERS

The ground feeder, as the name implies, involves placing the food (most often mixed birdseed) directly on the ground—usually grass, or snow in winter.

In my yard, the House Finch, Mourning Dove, Rufous-sided Towhee, California Towhee, California Thrasher, Scrub Jay, Dark-eyed Junco, Plain Titmouse, and White-crowned, Golden-crowned, Song, and House Sparrows all use my ground feeders from time to time.

Other birds that utilize ground feeders include the Black-capped Chickadee, Tufted Titmouse, European Starling, Northern Cardinal, White-throated Sparrow, Brown-headed Cowbird, and Rock Dove.

If you have a compost pile and you have mockingbirds in your neighborhood, they are almost certain to visit your compost pile regularly to pick out ants and other insects from the organic matter that is decaying there. They will eventually bring their fledglings down to your compost pile and teach these little puffballs the art of insect hunting.

It is important to place your ground feeder near flowers or shrubs where birds can quickly take cover from predators.

In my yard, I have dubbed the area of lawn in front of the flowering plum tree Towhee Corner, but all of my ground-feeding birds visit this area each day. The corner is bordered by a flowerbed containing turf lily, statice, daisies, azalea, and Mexican sage. Behind the flowerbed is a juniper tree, the flowering

plum, and a tall oleander bush that runs the length of the yard.

I usually spread mixed birdseed on the ground, but sometimes I also set aside a special area of the corner for cracked corn, which is readily eaten by all of my ground-feeding birds. This gives the birds a bit of variety.

I do not recommend putting bakery products such as doughnuts or bread (or other leftovers) on the ground, as these foods will probably attract squirrels and other rodents sooner or later.

Be sure to put out only as much birdseed as the birds can eat in a day or two. If you leave the seed out too long, it can become stale or moldy and can possibly cause harm to the birds. Also, make sure that you clean up your ground-feeder area regularly; and be sure to move the ground feeder around to different sections of the yard. In this way, all of the seed will either be eaten up or will work its way into the soil.

You may also want to place a piece of plywood out on the ground and spread out your birdseed on the plywood. In damp or snowy environments, this will help to keep your seed from getting wet and moldy. My House Finches and Mourning Doves clean me out of birdseed just as readily off the plywood as they do on the bare ground. Be sure to move the plywood around the yard regularly so that your lawn does not get damaged.

HOPPER FEEDERS

Hopper feeders consist of a central container, or hopper, through which the birdseed is dispensed to the birds. Hopper feeders come in many shapes and sizes and can be pole-mounted, hung from tree branches or horizontal wires, or even placed in your window by suction cups.

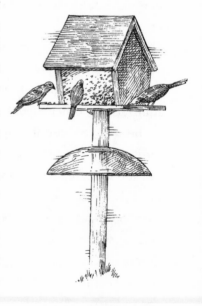

In my yard, I use two hopper feeders that are shaped like lanterns. One is hung on an outer branch of an apricot tree in the side yard and the other is mounted by suction cups on a picture window that surrounds an atrium and is visible from my kitchen table.

I usually fill my lantern feeders with mixed birdseed, and this attracts the House Finches all day long and often well into the evening. The perching area that surrounds the hopper gives the finches plenty of space to perch, and the inner tray holds more seed than any finch can eat in a single visit.

The clear plastic sides of the hopper allow me to see how much of the birdseed remains, and these walls along with the roof of the feeder protect the birdseed from the elements.

Since the perching area that surrounds the tray is only about six inches long, the Scrub Jay has a bit of trouble with the tightness of the feeding area, and it is amusing to watch him swing back and forth with the hanging lantern feeder, as his weight is enough to unbalance the feeder, whereas the finches are light enough not to make a difference.

Larger hopper feeders that are shaped like a house or barn provide better perching areas for larger birds such as the Scrub and Blue Jays; Evening, Rose-breasted, and Black-headed Grosbeaks; and the Northern Cardinal—but they are also popular with smaller birds such as the Red-breasted and White-

breasted Nuthatches; the Black-capped Chickadee; and the Pine Siskin.

TUBE FEEDERS

Tube feeders are basically hopper feeders that are shaped like a long tube and have a series of holes, or ports, through which the birds can access the seeds.

Most tube feeders are designed to serve mixed bird-seed or sunflower seeds to the birds, but some tube feeders are specially created to serve only sunflower seeds or, in the case of the American Goldfinch, Pine Siskin, and Common Redpoll, thistle seeds.

Some tube feeders include a tray at the bottom that will catch most of the extra seeds that the birds fling about. Still, inevitably, some of the birdseed finds its way to the ground, where it is readily consumed by ground-feeding birds such as the California Towhee and the Mourning Dove (both of which I have never seen at a tube feeder, although they will use platform feeders).

As with other hopper feeders, tube feeders can either be hung or mounted on poles. A squirrel baffle (a cone-shaped dome of clear plastic that tips when a squirrel applies its weight to it) can either be hung over the feeder or placed partway up the pole.

However, some tube feeders have metal caps, perches, and feeding ports that are virtually squirrel-resistant; and there is even an all-iron tube feeder that is not only squirrel-resistant but bear resistant as well!

And if you want to be sure that your House Finches do not use up your thistle seed, you can use a specially designed "upside-down" thistle feeder for your American Goldfinches, Pine Siskins, and Common Redpolls—which has its perches placed *above* the feeder ports. Thus, birds that can feed while hanging upside down can use this, but others cannot.

PLATFORM FEEDERS

Platform feeders, as the name implies, involve providing a raised platform on which the birds can feed. This platform can be anywhere from a foot or two off the ground to five or six feet high, depending on your wishes.

My first platform feeder consists of a wooden bench 15 inches wide, 19¾ inches long, and 18½ inches tall. The top of the bench has four slats, 3½ inches across and 1½ inches thick, with spaces of ½ inch between the slats. These spaces provide drainage for any water that might fall on the feeder from rain or sprinklers, and they also allow some of the seed to fall onto the ground for ground-feeding birds.

When I started my bird garden, I placed about one cup of mixed birdseed, thirty roasted, unshelled peanuts, a halved orange, and a halved apple on the feeder.

The orange and apple were for my mockingbird neighbor, who sang all day long from the top of the juniper tree next door, but I could not entice him down to the table.

What I did get, almost immediately, was a beautiful, blue Scrub Jay, who systematically cleaned me out of the peanuts, then the birdseed. Over the years on this platform feeder, I have fed this Scrub Jay along with his mate (and an assortment of other birds) everything from bread, graham crackers, doughnuts, black oil sunflower seeds, cracked corn, walnuts, and almonds to peanut butter and cornbread mixtures of various kinds.

I have also used my cement, pedestal birdbath as a platform feeder when it is not being used as a birdbath. It is nineteen inches in diameter (including a two-inch perching area) and about two feet high—and it holds a lot of birdseed!

To determine which foods were the most popular for my birds (and to give them some variety—a smorgasbord, as it were), I separated the feeding areas of the birdbath into black oil sunflower seeds; shelled sunflower hearts and chips; mixed birdseed; and cracked corn.

As I watched the Scrub Jays and House Finches devour the seeds from the birdbath, I discovered that the sunflowers (whether shelled or unshelled) were chosen first and were even picked out from the mixed birdseed. The rest of the mixed birdseed and the cracked corn were equally favored by the birds. I like to think that the cracked corn provides an enjoyable taste sensation for the birds, much as we like corn on the cob.

I like platform feeders because you can place them a fair distance from the house, so the birds are

in less danger of crashing into your windows. Furthermore, platform feeders attract a wide variety of birds, and although this results in more seed being used than in tube feeders, it is fun to watch so many birds feeding all at once—and it feels as if they are safer being raised off the ground.

Be sure to clean your platform feeders (and all your other feeders) regularly, and move them around the yard every few days so the seed that falls off the platforms to the ground does not suffocate any section of your lawn or cause any danger to your birds by becoming wet and moldy.

WINDOW FEEDERS

Window feeders provide a special pleasure by allowing you to observe your birds up close.

As I write this, I am watching two female House Finches eat the shelled sunflower hearts and chips from the lantern feeder that is attached to my picture window with suction cups.

The finches use the surrounding roof area of my atrium from which to foray to the feeder. My male Anna's Hummingbird, on the other hand, loves to perch in the tall bamboo branches in the center of the atrium, and he now considers the hummingbird feeder that is attached to the picture window as his property.

He spends almost all day from dawn until dusk between his perch and the feeder, and he chases away all interloping hummingbirds (including his neighbor out at the pool area) with his characteristic *zzz-zzz-zzz* sound. I enjoy sneaking up on him from next to the sliding door to the atrium, so that I am only inches away from him and I can see his throat move every time he swallows the sugar water from the feeder.

SUET FEEDERS

Suet feeders are designed to hold suet, or beef fat. Commercially available suet feeders consist of a wire basket that you can hang from a nearby tree branch. (It is best to hang suet feeders from trees or attach them to the trunks, as birds that look to trees for insects are often the same birds that utilize suet feeders.) You can also place suet in mesh bags, in pinecones, or in holes drilled into small logs.

Suet can be used directly as is, or it can be rendered, or melted, and have other ingredients—such as mixed birdseed, peanut butter, cornmeal, raisins, or various nuts—mixed in to form cakes.

Commercially available suet cakes are designed to fit into square, rectangular, or round suet baskets, but homemade suet mixtures can be placed into these baskets as well.

Since suet will melt or become rancid in warm weather, using suet feeders is primarily a wintertime activity, especially in the northern regions of North America.

Birds that use suet feeders include the Yellow-bellied Sapsucker; Downy and Hairy Woodpeckers; Northern Flicker; Blue and Scrub Jays; Black-capped and Carolina Chickadees; Tufted Titmouse; Red-breasted and White-breasted Nuthatches; Golden-crowned and Ruby-crowned Kinglets; Eastern Bluebird; Northern Mockingbird; Brown Thrasher; European Starling; Scarlet Tanager; and Purple and House Finches.

HUMMINGBIRD AND ORIOLE FEEDERS

No backyard bird garden would be complete without a hummingbird feeder or two (or three!), as well as an oriole feeder, if possible.

In my yard, I have at various times used a three-ounce hummingbird feeder that is shaped like a large test tube; an eight-ounce window feeder shaped like a circular feeder that has been sliced in half lengthwise; a sixteen-ounce feeder with three feeding stations; a forty-eight-ounce feeder shaped like a large apple; and an eight-ounce feeder shaped like a wildflower and placed on a pole.

Right now, I just keep my window feeder and sixteen-ounce feeder going for my two Anna's Hummingbirds, which manage to drink one-quarter to one-half cup of sugar water each day—per bird!

Add to this the consumption of my male, female, and immature Hooded Orioles, which together consume about one cup of sugar water each day, and you can see that preparing sugar water for my hummingbirds and orioles has become a daily task.

If you rub a good coat of vegetable oil on the hanger and the surrounding branch area (if your feeder is in a tree), ants will be discouraged from visiting your hummingbird and oriole feeders.

• • •

FEEDER CLEANING AND MAINTENANCE

No matter which type of birdfeeder you use, it is important to clean your feeders regularly. This will remove rotting food that may contain mold or bacteria and will also eliminate bird droppings from the feeding areas, which can also cause disease.

Hopper feeders, tube feeders, and hummingbird and oriole feeders should be cleaned in hot water. Hard to reach nooks and crannies can be cleaned with a bottlebrush or a toothbrush. Hopper and tube feeders should be cleaned monthly, while hummingbird and oriole feeders should in general be cleaned at least once each week, and at least every few days in hot weather.

To keep your bird food from spoiling, it is better to put out small amounts at regular intervals than to leave a big pile of birdseed outside to face the elements over a longer time. After a rain, I have discovered spoiled birdseed on the platform feeder underneath the seed on top, which has dried first. By the time the birds get down to this bottom layer of seed, it will be even more spoiled, so the best thing to do in this case is to discard all of the old birdseed and start over with fresh, dry birdseed. If you do not put out too much birdseed at any one time, you will not be forced to throw much of it away, if any—because the birds will have a chance to eat it before it goes bad.

The cleaner you keep your birdfeeders and the areas in which they are placed, the healthier and happier your birds will be—and the more successful your backyard bird garden will become.

SQUIRRELS AND OTHER PESTS

Sooner or later, all bird gardeners have to resign themselves to sharing some of their birdseed with squirrels. Chances are that you will have to contend with either the Eastern or Western Gray Squirrel, the Fox Squirrel, or the Red Squirrel, depending on where in North America you live.

In nature, squirrels eat nuts such as acorns and walnuts, pine seeds from pinecones, various fruits and berries, as well as tree buds, flowers, mushrooms, insects, and lichen, among other things. But if you present a tray full of sunflower seeds, peanut-butter mixtures, cracked or whole corn, or even suet, you will no doubt attract squirrels to your refreshments, as well as the birds you desire.

To keep squirrels away from your bird feeders, you can use one or both of two basic strategies: provide extra, diversionary food for the squirrels, or keep the squirrels from getting at your feeders.

Some people actually enjoy feeding squirrels and watching their antics, and many wild-bird catalogs and stores offer an assortment of products that will allow you to do just that.

There are tables with spikes on which you can attach ears of corn; simply attach the table to a tree or fence post. Another product consists of a wheel on which five ears of corn are attached; the wheel spins as the squirrels jump from ear to ear.

You could also just sprinkle some cracked corn or bread on the ground to keep the squirrels away from your sunflower feeders.

To protect your feeder, the most common method is to place a dome-shaped squirrel baffle above the feeder, so that the squirrel slips on the baffle's plastic or metal surface and falls to the ground.

A cone-shaped metal baffle can also be placed partway up a pole on which a feeder is mounted. Just be sure that the baffle is at least four feet off the ground, so that the squirrels cannot jump over it; and be sure that the feeder is at least ten feet away from any nearby tree or eave, as squirrels have incredible leaping ability. You can also purchase a metal tubular baffle that will fit around your birdfeeder post and will keep not only squirrels but raccoons from reaching your prized sunflower seeds in the feeders above.

Another squirrel deterrent is a metal cage that can be placed around the feeder and allows smaller birds such as chickadees, finches, and titmice in, while keeping squirrels and larger "nuisance" birds such as starlings and grackles out. These metal cages can be purchased separately to be placed around your older feeders, or you can purchase them already built into a new feeder. There is even a specially designed suet cage that will protect your suet from squirrels as well!

Yet another ingenious squirrel-proof feeder features a weight-sensitive surface that automatically closes the feeder ports when a heavy object such as a squirrel arrives, while allowing light objects such as birds to feed with impunity. A similar model actually causes the perches to tilt toward the ground when a squirrel lands on one, thus causing the squirrel to fall to the ground as well.

Meanwhile, if you hang your feeders from a taut wire that is attached to two tree limbs or the eaves of a house, you can protect those feeders from the squirrels by placing lengths of garden hose, spools of thread, 35mm film canisters, plastic soda bottles, milk jugs, or coffee cans along the wire, thus causing the squirrels either to retreat with dignity or to lose their footing and fall to the ground, foiled again.

In addition to squirrels, you may have some other

unwelcome guests in your bird garden that are much more dangerous for your birds—namely, hawks and cats.

Both the Sharp-shinned Hawk and the Cooper's Hawk are common throughout most of North America, and these woodland raptors will occasionally prey on an unsuspecting or infirm backyard bird such as a junco or sparrow.

To protect your birds from such unwelcome attacks, provide plenty of nearby trees, shrubs, and brush piles in which the birds can take cover and from which they can observe the surrounding area and call out a warning to their friends, if a hawk does indeed appear.

However, by weeding out the sick birds from the population, the hawks actually help to prevent the spread of infection and disease that can occur when large groups of birds flock together, as they do in our backyard gardens.

Cats are especially dangerous to birds during nesting season, when juvenile birds (who cannot yet fly well) and low-lying nests provide the easiest targets. However, adult birds are also potential meals for cats, so the best way to protect your birds is to keep your cats indoors at all times. You can also equip your cat's collar with a bell—and be sure that your feeders and birdbaths are elevated off the ground and are far enough away from nearby perches so that cats cannot pounce on the birds. Also, clear out your nearby shrubs so cats cannot hide in them and birds can have a good view of a possible predator lurking there.

AND NOW,
FOR THE FOOD . . .

Once you have your birdfeeders in place, you have to fill them up with the specific types of bird food that will appeal to the specific birds that will visit your garden.

That is the subject of our next chapter.

CHAPTER
THREE

Bird Foods

FOOD, OF COURSE, is at the heart of your backyard bird garden.

Birds eat seeds and grains, nuts, fruits, bakery products, suet, sugar water, and even such items as baked potatoes, cooked rice, and cheese.

In my garden, I have also devised a number of peanut-butter and cornmeal mixtures that appeal to my birds—especially my voracious, entertaining Scrub Jays.

When you start your bird garden, you will no doubt use one of the many birdseed mixtures that are on the market.

BIRDSEED MIXES

Birdseed mixes generally contain white and/or red proso millet, milo, cracked corn, wheat, and sunflower seeds.

Some premium, or gourmet, birdseed mixes include sunflower seeds, millet, and cracked corn, but also include peanuts, sunflower hearts, safflower seed, thistle seed, or even such fruits as raisins and dried cherries, apples, and raspberries.

Seed mixtures for small birds such as House Finches and Pine Siskins include small seeds such as red and white proso millet, thistle seed, canary grass seed, flaxseed, and hulled sunflower chips.

Some seed mixtures that produce no waste include hulled sunflower pieces, red and white proso millet, cracked corn, peanuts, and canary grass seed. This type of seed mix is excellent for use on a patio or in an atrium, where you want to keep your seed mess to a minimum.

Perhaps the most popular bird food is sunflower hearts and chips, which can be purchased as a special mix. Most birds like sunflower seeds, and for those that do, these already hulled sunflower seeds are almost impossible to resist. They also produce no mess.

Other bird foods that can be purchased separately include black oil and striped sunflower seed, thistle seed, cracked corn, and safflower seed.

It is fun to create your own birdseed mix, or to put some of these ingredients out separately for the birds. I especially enjoy adding extra black oil sunflower seeds to a regular birdseed mixture, as my Scrub Jays and House Finches always devour any sunflower seeds in these mixes before moving on to the millet, milo, and cracked corn.

Indeed, black oil sunflower seeds are more popular with my birds than striped sunflower seeds. For one thing, oil sunflower seeds are smaller and easier for the birds to crack open, and secondly, they contain more oil and meat per seed. No wonder my black oil sunflower seeds tend to disappear almost as soon as I put them out in the yard, while the striped sunflower seeds usually remain untouched a while longer. Still, any sunflower seed (or part thereof) is more effective for attracting birds than just about any other food.

NUTS

Nuts for your birds include peanuts, almonds, walnuts, and pecans. My Scrub Jays have eaten all of these nuts, but they are especially fond of peanuts. I have served my jays raw, unshelled peanuts; roasted, unshelled peanuts; roasted, unsalted peanut kernels; and peanut-butter mixtures. They love it all.

One day, shortly after starting my bird garden, I spread about one hundred unshelled, roasted peanuts out amid the mixed birdseed at a six-foot-by-three-foot-long ground feeder in the side yard. It took my pair of Scrub Jays about an hour to clean me out of peanuts. Sometimes, they picked up two peanuts in their mouth and flew off to eat and/or store them.

When all of the peanuts were gone, the male Scrub Jay perched in the palm tree and began screeching at me—"Screech, screech, screech!" That is, "Where are all the peanuts? What is going on?"

Since the jays had just taken fifty peanuts each, I knew that it was not hunger that was driving this jay to yell at me. Was it a game? Was he disappointed that he could not fly down and pick up the peanuts anymore?

I did not want to take the chance of losing my goodwill with my new friends, so I threw a peanut out to the ground feeder, and the Scrub Jay flew right down, picked it up in his beak, and flew out of the yard with glee. The game was on, and he has been in the yard ever since.

Just as the Scrub Jay collects peanuts, he collects black oil sunflower seeds, sometimes holding as many as fifteen seeds in his mouth and beak before flying off. It looks as if he is swallowing the seeds whole, but he is not. When his mouth is full, he picks up a line of seeds in his beak, sometimes pausing to get one extra seed that is virtually hanging from a thread at the end of this line of seeds. How he knows that he can fit that extra seed in his bill is beyond me.

FRUITS

When it comes to fruit, backyard birds have eclectic tastes.

For instance, the Gray Catbird eats bananas, grapes, oranges, and raisins; the House Finch eats apples, bananas, grapes, and watermelon; the Northern Mockingbird eats apples, bananas, grapes, oranges, watermelon, and raisins; and the Northern Oriole eats apples, grapes, oranges, watermelon, and raisins.

Meanwhile, the Cedar Waxwing and American Robin eat apples, grapes, and raisins; the Yellow-breasted Chat eats apples and bananas; the Western Tanager eats bananas, grapes, and oranges; the Rose-breasted Grosbeak eats grapes, oranges, and watermelon; the Brown Thrasher eats oranges and raisins; and the Hairy Woodpecker eats apples and grapes.

For presentation, apples and oranges can be halved and impaled on branches or nails around the yard, or placed on platform feeders. Large pieces of banana can be impaled in this fashion, too, or cut up for platform feeders. Raisins should be softened in water or steamed.

You might want to present a fruit cocktail for your birds, consisting of cut-up apples, oranges, bananas, and watermelon, along with cherries, grapes, and perhaps some dried fruit that has been soaked in water to soften it up. Place your fruit cocktail in a bowl, in an empty orange or grapefruit half, in a hollowed-out watermelon shell, or simply place these delectables directly on your platform feeder.

By experimentation and observation, you will discover which birds in your area prefer which fruits that you provide them.

Perhaps one fine day, you will see a White-crowned Sparrow, Curve-billed Thrasher, Hermit or Varied Thrush, Orange-crowned Warbler, or Cactus Wren fly into your yard for your apples; or a Scarlet Tanager, Yellow-rumped Warbler, or Red-bellied Woodpecker fly in for your oranges; or a Black-headed Grosbeak, Scott's Oriole, Swainson's Thrush, or Acorn Woodpecker drift down out of the sky to sample some of your grapes.

BAKED PRODUCTS

In addition to fruits, birds are fond of a variety of baked products, from wheat bread to corn bread, from bagels to graham crackers, from doughnuts to cookies.

In my garden, the California Towhees take my bread from ground feeders and platform feeders— whether it is soggy or not, whether it is white bread or wheat bread. They just like bread.

The Rufous-sided Towhees and Scrub Jays like to eat bread, too, and while the House Finches will eat bread, as a rule they favor the seeds and grains over baked products.

It is best to present bread in small pieces or as bread crumbs. This way, the birds can take the bread quickly and either eat it on the spot, as the jays usually do, or carry it in their beaks into the bushes or to another sheltered spot away from the yard, as the California and Rufous-sided Towhees do. It is quite a sight to see a California Towhee flying over my pool and into the canyon with a light-colored piece of bread sticking out of his dark brown bill. One can only imagine the delight he has in eating his bread in the comfort of his own shelter—wherever that is.

But perhaps the biggest bakery hit in my yard was the sugar-and-cinnamon-covered graham crackers I put out on the platform feeder one day in late May. Once the Scrub Jays and California Towhees tasted these graham crackers, they took away as many as I could put out. Sometimes a jay would gather two or three one-inch-square pieces in its mouth and fly off proudly with its cache. If I softened up these pieces with water, the jays could peck sections of the graham crackers right off the platform feeder and eat them on the spot. Talk about a sweet tooth!

PEANUT-BUTTER AND CORNMEAL MIXTURES

But even these graham-cracker delights paled in comparison with the glee with which my Scrub Jays and California Towhees attacked my peanut-butter and cornmeal mixtures—which I placed on my bench platform feeder. (It is important to mix peanut butter with other ingredients such as cornmeal, suet, or oats, as it is possible for birds to choke on pure peanut butter.)

The first mixture I devised consists of three ounces of cornmeal mixed with one ounce of peanut butter. After mixing these ingredients together in a bowl, I molded a three-inch-diameter patty out of it and placed this tannish yellow "burger" on the platform feeder (see Box 1, Peanut-Butter and Cornmeal Mixture I).

Within moments, my Scrub Jay and one of his fledglings were taking turns at pecking (or was it tearing?) huge chunks of the mixture out from the patty and either gobbling up these chunks on the spot or flying off to a hidden perch with a full bill.

Shortly thereafter, the California Towhee got in on the action, taking as many as twenty small bites of the mixture at a visit, then flying off with a mouthful for himself.

BOX 1

PEANUT-BUTTER
AND CORNMEAL MIXTURES

❧

PEANUT-BUTTER AND CORNMEAL
MIXTURE I

3 ounces cornmeal
1 ounce peanut butter

Mix the cornmeal and peanut butter together in a bowl. Mold this mixture into a patty. *Makes ½ cup.*

PEANUT-BUTTER AND CORNMEAL
MIXTURE II

3 ounces cornmeal
½ ounce peanut butter
½ ounce vegetable shortening, melted suet, or lard

Mix all the ingredients together in a bowl. Mold this mixture into a patty. *Makes ½ cup.*

PEANUT-BUTTER AND CORNMEAL
MIXTURE III

3 ounces cornmeal
½ ounce peanut butter
½ ounce vegetable shortening, melted suet, or lard
1 ounce mixed birdseed
1 ounce black oil sunflower seeds

Mix all the ingredients except the sunflower seeds together in a bowl. Mold this mixture into a patty, then roll the patty in the sunflower seeds, pressing to be sure that the sunflower seeds stick to the patty. *Makes ¾ cup.*

My success encouraged me to try other mixtures. First, I used three ounces of cornmeal as before, but this time I added one-half ounce of peanut butter and one-half ounce of vegetable shortening to the mixture and molded it into a patty and placed the patty on the platform feeder (see Box 1, Peanut-Butter and Cornmeal Mixture II).

Then I made another mixture like this one, but I added one ounce of mixed birdseed to the mixture, molded it into a patty, then rolled the patty in one ounce of black oil sunflower seeds, pressing to be sure that the seeds stuck to the patty (see Box 1, Peanut-Butter and Cornmeal Mixture III).

The Scrub Jays and California Towhees took to these two mixtures as well, but the sunflower seeds attracted them to the second mixture more often than the first mixture—and the sunflower seeds along with the mixed birdseed also attracted the House Finches to the second mixture. However, the House Finches are not as fond of these basic mixtures as they are of their favorite seeds.

BOX 2

SWEET CORNMEAL MIXTURES

 ❧

SWEET CORNMEAL MIXTURE

1 cup water
1 ounce vegetable shortening, melted suet, or lard
½ cup cornmeal
1 ounce white, granulated sugar

Bring the water and shortening, suet, or lard to a boil in a saucepan. Remove from heat and stir the cornmeal and sugar into the water. Allow the mixture to cool, then mold it into 2 patties. *Makes about 1 cup*

VARIATIONS

For a Walnut Sweet Cornmeal Mixture, stir ½ cup chopped walnuts along with the cornmeal and sugar into the water. Proceed as directed above.

For a Peanut Butter Sweet Cornmeal Mixture, stir 1 ounce peanut butter along with the cornmeal and sugar into the water. Proceed as directed above.

For a Mixed Birdseed Sweet Cornmeal Mixture, stir ½ cup mixed birdseed along with the cornmeal and sugar into the water. Proceed as directed above.

For a Cracked Corn Sweet Cornmeal Mixture, add ½ cup cracked corn along with the cornmeal and sugar into the water. Proceed as directed above.

(You can stuff peanut-butter mixtures into holes in suet logs, into pinecones, or you can spread them on tree trunks as well. Perhaps you will attract a Downy or Hairy Woodpecker, Northern Flicker, Black-capped Chickadee, Tree Sparrow, Dark-eyed Junco, Golden-crowned Kinglet, Northern Mockingbird, Orange-crowned Warbler, Carolina Wren, Blue Jay, Brown Creeper, Wood Thrush, Bushtit, or Wrentit to your peanut-butter mixture someday, as all of these birds love peanut butter.)

SWEET CORNMEAL MIXTURES

Next, I made a series of sweet cornmeal mixtures (see Box 2). These patties all look a little bit different. The basic mixture is a pale yellow; the walnut mixture is light brown; the peanut butter mixture is tan; the birdseed mixture has speckles of millet, milo, and black oil sunflower seeds; and the cracked-corn mixture has yellow bits of cracked corn sticking out of it.

But whatever the color, the birds took to these sweet patties in a big way—no matter what the variation. The Scrub Jays took big chunks out of all of the patties, sometimes dropping pieces of the mixture on the ground in their excitement, then going after them. The California Towhees seemed to prefer the peanut-butter variation (although they ate them all), while the House Finches picked the mixed birdseed and black oil sunflower seeds out of the mixed-birdseed variation, as usual.

SUET

Suet, or beef fat, can be served to birds either as is or in rendered form.

To render suet, simply cut it up into small chunks or put it through a meat grinder. Then melt it over low heat in a pan (or in a microwave oven). Allow the suet to cool and solidify, then reheat the suet again until it is liquid. Allow it to cool a second time, but before it solidifies, stir in the birdseed, peanut butter, cornmeal, raisins, nuts, or whatever else you want to add to it.

Pour the suet into molds such as tuna-fish or frozen-orange-juice cans, or into muffin pans or directly into holes in small logs. During warm weather, store your suet in the refrigerator when it is not being used outside for the birds.

Commercially available suet cakes come in a variety of flavors, including peanut, orange, cherry, raisin, and almond. You can also purchase suet cakes that contain mixed birdseed, sunflower seeds, berries, or insects—and you can even purchase rendered-beef-suet cakes without anything added to them at all.

Suet dough cakes, which contain assorted grains to keep the suet from melting, are also available in various flavors, for use in warmer climates.

BIRDSEED BELLS

In addition to suet cakes such as these, you can also purchase birdseed bells, which consist of various types of birdseed that are held together by an adhesive and form the shape of a bell. You can hang these bells throughout your garden.

In my yard, the House Finches are fond of the mixed-birdseed and black-oil-sunflower-seed bells and can often be seen hanging rightside up or upside down on these bells and pecking away at the seeds that are stuck to them. The Scrub Jays will hang on the bells and feed from time to time as well, especially when there is little food elsewhere in the garden.

Therefore, the bells are a good source of backup food in the garden—and they are also available with thistle seed, peanut butter, and even dried berries on them.

HUMMINGBIRD AND ORIOLE NECTAR

To prepare sugar water for your hummingbirds and orioles, simply boil one part white, granulated sugar in four or five parts water for a couple of minutes. Allow this mixture to cool before filling your feeders, and store the remaining sugar water in the refrigerator. It will keep safely for about a week.

Commercially available nectar mixes for hummingbirds and orioles can also be used; simply stir the powder into regular tap water and fill up your feeders. *Never* use honey in your nectar solution, as honey can produce a fungus that is fatal to hummingbirds and orioles.

GRIT

Since birds do not have teeth, they grind up their food in their gizzards by using grinding agents such as small pebbles, sand, charcoal, ashes, and bits of soil. By providing grit for our birds, we can help them with their digestion and also supply them with some much needed salt and minerals. This is especially helpful in winter, when most of the naturally available grit is buried under the snow.

In my yard, I use commercially available "high calcium grit," which contains such ingredients as granite grit, oyster shell, calcium carbonate, salt, and charcoal. I place small amounts of this grit periodically on my platform feeder, away from the birdseed, and I notice that the birds regularly use it. You can also mix your grit in with your birdseed, but I like to give the birds the option of eating their seeds separately.

Another source of grit (and calcium) is crushed eggshells, which you can leave out separately for your birds or mix in with their birdseed. Eggshells are especially valuable as a source of grit for Purple Martins, who spend most of their time on the wing chasing down and eating insects and who eschew other forms of grit.

OBSERVE WHAT YOUR BIRDS EAT

In the end, a little bit of observation will go a long way toward helping you provide the most popular foods for the birds in your garden.

For instance, my Scrub Jays have eaten doughnuts, bagels, waffles, Swiss cheese, corn bread, and even chocolate-covered peanuts. Meanwhile, the House Finches usually ignore bakery products, but will eat thistle seed and cracked corn in addition to their mixed birdseed and sunflower seeds. The California Towhee, on the other hand, loves bakery products, millet, milo, and cracked corn, but is not as big a fan of the unshelled sunflower seeds as the House Finch. The Rufous-sided Towhee has similar tastes to the California Towhee, while the Mourning Dove virtually ignores the unshelled sunflower seeds and eats almost exclusively small seeds such as millet, proso, and cracked corn.

Of course, the reward for providing the right food for your birds is that you get to see the birds themselves.

In another sense, however, you are contributing to the survival of nature—and what could be more noble than that?

POPULAR BIRDS AND THEIR FAVORITE FOODS

The following list presents the favorite foods of some of our most popular birds.

Doves, Pigeons—millet, cracked corn, thistle, milo, peanut and sunflower hearts, bread.

Woodpeckers—suet, sunflower seeds, peanuts, fruit, corn bread.

Jays—peanuts, sunflower seeds, cracked corn, suet, raisins, bread.

Chickadees, Titmice—sunflower seeds, peanuts, suet, safflower seeds, baked goods.

Nuthatches—sunflower seeds, peanuts, suet, fruit, baked goods.

Wrens—suet, peanut-butter mixtures, bread.

Bluebirds, Thrushes, Robins—peanuts, raisins, suet, cracked corn, fruit, bread.

Catbirds, Mockingbirds, Thrashers—fruit, suet, peanut-butter mixtures, raisins, cracked corn, doughnuts.

Waxwings—fruit, raisins, sunflower seeds.

Starlings—cracked corn, peanuts, fruit, raisins, suet, baked goods.

Tanagers—fruit, suet, bread, sugar water.

Cardinals—sunflower seeds, safflower seeds, peanuts, cracked corn, millet, milo, suet.

Grosbeaks—sunflower seeds, cracked corn, peanuts, suet.

Towhees—sunflower seeds, cracked corn, millet, milo, peanuts, bread.

Juncos—sunflower seeds, millet, thistle, cracked corn, peanuts, bread.

Sparrows—sunflower seeds, millet, cracked corn, milo, peanuts, bread.

Blackbirds—cracked corn, sunflower seeds, millet, peanuts, bread.

Orioles—fruit, sugar water, suet, raisins.

Finches—sunflower seeds, millet, milo, thistle, peanuts, suet.

Goldfinches—thistle, sunflower seeds, peanuts, suet.

Plantings

BIRDS, OF COURSE, are perfectly capable of surviving in nature without the help of man. Birds utilize trees, shrubs, vines, flowers, and grasses as sources of food, shelter, and nesting sites.

By providing a wide selection of the plantings that birds like, and in the right places, you can provide your birds with an environment that approximates what they use in nature.

In this way, you will increase the probability of your birds not only passing through your yard to grab a seed from a feeder, but remaining in your yard from year to year as residents or seasonal visitors.

TREES

Birds use trees for seeds, fruit, and even acorns.

Fir trees, for instance, provide seeds for the Black-capped Chickadee, Dark-eyed Junco, Scrub Jay, Red-breasted Nuthatch, and California Towhee.

Maple trees provide seeds for the Evening Grosbeak, Purple Finch, and Pine Siskin, while spruce trees provide seeds for these birds along with the Black-capped Chickadee, Red-breasted Nuthatch, and Cedar Waxwing.

Meanwhile, pine trees provide seeds for the Red

Crossbill; Downy and Hairy Woodpeckers; and Scrub, Blue, and Steller's Jays.

Alder, birch, and larch trees are also popular seed-providers for birds such as the Mourning Dove, Rufous-sided Towhee, and American Goldfinch respectively.

But trees can also be a great source of life-sustaining fruits and berries for birds, especially in fall and winter.

The berry of the juniper, or red cedar, tree attracts not only the aptly named Cedar Waxwing, but the Northern Cardinal, Evening Grosbeak, American Robin, and Eastern and Western Bluebirds as well.

Meanwhile, the fruit of the mulberry tree attracts all of these birds, as well as the House and Purple Finches, Brown Thrasher, Scarlet Tanager, Wood Thrush, and Downy Woodpecker. And the red berries of the mountain ash attract bluebirds, waxwings, grosbeaks, and robins, as well as the Gray Catbird.

The fruits of the hawthorn, cherry, and crab apple trees are also enjoyed by such birds as the Scrub and Blue Jays, Song and White-throated Sparrows, and Purple and House Finches respectively.

Acorns from oak trees are enjoyed by a wide assortment of birds, including the appropriately named Acorn Woodpecker, Tufted Titmouse, Black-capped Chickadee, White-breasted Nuthatch, Evening Grosbeak, and Steller's Jay.

SHRUBS

In addition to your fruit-bearing trees, there are a number of fruit-bearing shrubs that birds enjoy.

The most popular of these shrubs include serviceberry, holly, dogwood, barberry, bayberry, beauty-berry, cotoneaster, pyracantha, viburnum, and brambles.

Birds such as cardinals, bluebirds, waxwings, robins, catbirds, grosbeaks, mockingbirds, finches, sparrows, towhees, and thrushes are fond of berries produced by shrubs such as these.

VINES

A few well-placed vines will provide food for your birds, as well as shelter and nesting opportunities.

Virginia creeper, for instance, provides berries for bluebirds, robins, chickadees, and mockingbirds; grapevines produce grapes for jays, cardinals, finches, and towhees; and honeysuckle provides berries for such birds as thrushes and catbirds, as well as nectar for hummingbirds.

ANNUALS AND PERENNIALS

Seed-eating birds such as finches, goldfinches, cardinals, sparrows, chickadees, nuthatches, towhees, titmice, and doves will take advantage of seed-producing annuals such as sunflower, ageratum, sweet alyssum, marigold, zinnia, coreopsis, cosmos, and cornflower; as well as seed-producing perennials such as aster, purple coneflower, goldenrod, foxglove, columbine, and gloriosa daisy.

• • •

GRASS

If you let your grass grow, birds such as doves, sparrows, finches, and juncos will take advantage of your grass seed for sustenance.

HUMMINGBIRD FLOWERS

Flowers that provide nectar for hummingbirds include sage, coralbells, monkey flower, cardinal flower, penstemon, phlox, bee balm, columbine, foxglove, impatiens, red-hot poker, gilia, and bird-of-paradise; shrubs include fuchsia, lavender, butterfly bush, Chinese lantern, abelia, beauty bush, red-flowering currant, bottlebrush, and weigela; trees include eucalyptus, coral tree, acacia, silk tree, and citrus; and vines include trumpet creeper, honeysuckle, lantana, and flame fine.

PLANTS FOR INSECTS

Most birds eat insects as a major, if not the predominant, part of their diet. Swallows and Purple

Martins will catch insects such as flies, wasps, and beetles on the wing, while woodpeckers, nuthatches, and Brown Creepers climb along tree trunks looking for insects and spiders. Indeed, while the woodpeckers and Brown Creepers only climb up the tree trunks, the nuthatches can climb up as well as down the trunks and therefore find many insects that the woodpeckers and Brown Creepers miss.

Birds such as chickadees, titmice, bushtits, kinglets, sapsuckers, vireos, warblers, and chats forage for insects in trees, bushes, and hedges; while such birds as the Northern Flicker, Northern Mockingbird, European Starling, Rufous-sided Towhee, and Dark-eyed Junco find their insects in lawns or by scratching at dead leaves or the soil.

Therefore, by planting a good combination of trees, shrubs, vines, and ground cover that attract insects, you can also feed your birds with the insects that thrive on these plants.

For instance, the Yellow-bellied Sapsucker drills holes in the trunks of older trees for the sap that lies just under the bark—and it eats the sap as well as the insects that are drawn to the sap to feed themselves.

Meanwhile, insect-eating birds such as chickadees, bushtits, and warblers forage on the insects and spiders that they find in the foliage of birch and hawthorn trees.

Other trees that attract insects for birds include fir, dogwood, and oak, while insect-attracting shrubs include buckthorn, viburnum, and manzanita. Vines such as honeysuckle are also popular insect-attracting plants. In the case of honeysuckle, your hummingbirds will not only be able to drink from its nectar, but will also partake of the insects that they find on this beautiful vine.

PLANTS FOR SHELTER

When it comes to providing shelter for your birds, be sure to plant a good combination of trees, shrubs, and vines of varying heights. A nice hedge can be created with a mixture of shrubs and small trees. This can serve as a windbreak and as a refuge for roosting as well as nesting birds. It is best to place tall trees along the perimeter of your yard. If you place your tall trees behind your lower trees and shrubs, you can create a multilayered windbreak, and if you plant a variety of deciduous and evergreen trees and shrubs, you can be sure to have sheltering vegetation for your birds at all times of the year.

Many shelter trees for birds also provide food for them, such as the seed-bearing fir, maple, alder, birch, larch, spruce, pine, and hemlock—not to mention the acorn-bearing oak. The fruiting hackberry, hawthorn, holly, juniper, mulberry, cherry, sassafras, and mountain ash trees also provide good sheltering locations for birds.

As far as shrubs are concerned, the fruit-bearing barberry, dogwood, cotoneaster, mahonia, bayberry, firethorn, raspberry, elderberry, and viburnum all offer excellent shelter for birds.

If you plant pine trees, American Robins, Mourning Doves, Northern Cardinals, and Black-capped Chickadees will seek shelter among their needles, pinecones, and branches. The lower-lying juniper might shelter a combination of juncos, sparrows, and grosbeaks, and the even lower hawthorn might offer a safe haven for waxwings, jays, and mockingbirds.

Even closer to the ground, a group of cardinals or grosbeaks might join the waxwings, jays, and mockingbirds in the shelter of an elderberry bush—and if you search through an even lower-lying cotoneaster bush, you might just find a group of bluebirds, thrushes, or sparrows.

Some plants, such as hawthorn and rose, feature thorny stems that protect birds well and ward off predators. The needlelike leaves and stiff branches of the juniper serve a similar function, and the dense stems and foliage of blackberries and raspberries also offer great hiding places for birds such as cardinals, robins, and sparrows.

In addition, a number of vines offer excellent sheltering locations for birds, especially the twisting branches of the honeysuckle, Virginia creeper, and American bittersweet, as well as the canopy of a grapevine. And each of these vines also provides valuable fruit for such birds as woodpeckers, thrushes, catbirds, vireos, warblers, and robins.

PLANTS FOR NESTING

To raise a successful brood of fledglings, adult birds require a well-protected place in which to nest. While some birds nest in the tall trees, others set up homekeeping in shrubs, vines, and thickets, and other birds actually build their nests on the ground among the grasses, leaves, and twigs that they find there.

Birds that nest in conifers such as pine, fir, spruce, juniper, and hemlock include finches, warblers, juncos, robins, jays, grosbeaks, doves, and tanagers. Hummingbirds also use conifers for their nests, placing their delicate treasures on a low-lying branch. Other popular trees that birds use for their nests include oak, maple, hackberry, sycamore, elm, holly, and hawthorn.

Birds such as cardinals, mockingbirds, catbirds, towhees, sparrows, buntings, and thrashers build their nests in shrubs such as rose, blackberry, raspberry, and elderberry, or in vines such as honeysuckle. Hummingbirds often nest in trumpet creeper vines as well, which doubles as a favorite nectar source.

Some species of birds, such as the White-throated Sparrow, Song Sparrow, and Dark-eyed Junco, often build their nests right on the ground, although they will also use bushes and vines as the other birds do. Thus, it is important to leave plenty of leaves, twigs, and grasses on the ground for these birds to utilize in building their nests, as well as for the other birds, too.

Cavity-nesting birds, such as woodpeckers, carve out their nesting holes with their chisel-like bills into trees such as cottonwood, oak, and pine, or into cacti such as saguaro. Chickadees, titmice, and nuthatches also excavate nesting cavities in trees in their respective environments, and they often utilize abandoned woodpecker nests for their own. Other birds that use abandoned woodpecker nests and other cavities for their own nests include bluebirds, swallows, wrens, and owls. Therefore, having plenty of trees on your property (including dead trees) will go a long way in providing nesting locations for bird species such as those listed above.

POPULAR BIRDS AND PLANTS

Although many birds and the plants they use are common throughout North America, a great number of birds and their associated plants often occur in certain regions (while they may still occur elsewhere as well).

In the Northeast, birds such as the Ruby-throated Hummingbird, Pileated Woodpecker, Black-capped Chickadee, Red-breasted Nuthatch, Scarlet Tanager, and Red-breasted Grosbeak use trees such as fir *(Abies)*, birch *(Betula)*, maple *(Acer)*, and mountain ash *(Sorbus)*; shrubs such as cranberry bush *(Viburnum trilobum)*, rose *(Rosa)*, winterberry *(Ilex verticillata)*, and red-osier dogwood *(Cornus stolonifera)*; and vines such as grape *(Vitis)*.

In the Southeast, birds such as the Red-headed Woodpecker, Tree Swallow, Brown-headed Nuthatch, White-eyed Vireo, Summer Tanager, and Carolina Chickadee use trees such as magnolia *(Magnolia)*, persimmon *(Diospyros virginiana)*, tupelo *(Nyssa sylvatica)*, and hickory *(Carya)*; shrubs such as beauty-berry *(Callicarpa)*, spicebush *(Lindera)*, sumac *(Rhus)*, and bayberry *(Myrica pensylvanica)*; and vines such as supplejack *(Berchemia scandens)*.

In the Great Plains states, birds such as the Indigo Bunting, Lark Bunting, Yellow-headed Blackbird, Lark Sparrow, Dickcissel, and Orchard Oriole use trees such as Russian olive *(Elaeagnus angustifolia)*, arborvitae *(Thuja)*, common hackberry *(Celtis occidentalis)*, and cottonwood *(Populus)*; shrubs such as red chokeberry *(Aronia arbutifolia)*, western sand cherry *(Prunus besseyi)*, currant *(Ribes)*, and silver buffaloberry *(Shepherdia argentea)*; and vines such as Virginia creeper *(Parthenocissus quinquefolia)*.

In the Mountain states, birds such as the Black-billed Magpie, Broad-tailed Hummingbird, Pygmy Nuthatch, Mountain Bluebird, Mountain Chickadee, and Pine Grosbeak use trees such as alder *(Alnus)*, larch *(Larix)*, spruce *(Picea)*, and hemlock *(Tsuga)*; shrubs such as buckthorn *(Rhamnus)*, snowberry

(Symphoricarpos), photinia *(Photinia)*, and elder-berry *(Sambucus)*; and vines such as American bit-tersweet *(Celastrus scandens)*.

In the Pacific states, birds such as the Anna's Hummingbird, California Quail, California Towhee, Golden-crowned Sparrow, Western Bluebird, and Varied Thrush use trees such as madrone *(Arbutus menziesii)*, coast live oak *(Quercus agrifolia)*, Monterey pine *(Pinus radiata)*, and American sweet gum *(Liquidambar styraciflua)*; shrubs such as toyon *(Heteromeles arbutifolia)*, manzanita *(Arctostaphylos)*, serviceberry *(Amelanchier)*, and Oregon grape *(Mahonia aquifolium)*; and vines such as honeysuckle *(Lonicera)*.

DESIGNING YOUR GARDEN

Once you have decided which plants you are going to provide for your birds, it is important to place them in the appropriate manner to provide the best habitat for the birds to feed, perch, and perhaps even nest.

Most successful bird gardens feature a row of trees or hedges that provide protection from the wind and, in combination with flowerbeds and lawns, approximate a forest-edge environment. This allows birds to forage for food in the open areas and then retreat to the "woods" to nest and to roost.

Birds that will take advantage of a forest-edge habitat include the Evening Grosbeak, Downy and Hairy Woodpeckers, Northern Flicker, Scrub and Blue Jays, Dark-eyed Junco, Black-capped Chickadee, Red-eyed Vireo, Red-breasted and White-breasted Nuthatches, Gray Catbird, and Indigo Bunting. The part of your garden that approximates the habitat of open fields, brushlands, or orchards, with isolated groves of bushes and trees, will attract birds such as the American Goldfinch, Northern Oriole, Purple Martin, and Eastern and Western Meadowlarks; whereas generalists such as the American Robin, House Finch, Common Grackle, and Brown-headed Cowbird will thrive in a wide variety of habitats, from forests to fields to suburban backyards.

In my yard, a twelve-by-thirty-six-foot rectangle of lawn is bordered by a three-foot-wide bed of flowers and shrubs, which is backed on one side by an oleander hedge and on the other by the house.

On windy days, this sheltered area is like a quiet cocoon, where my birds and I while away the hours.

The hummingbird flowers bordering my yard include deep purple Mexican sage; pink azalea; blue lily-of-the-Nile; yellow gladiolus; English lavender; red and white varieties of geranium; purple and orange varieties of lantana; purple-and-pink fuchsia; white apricot; and pinkish purple star clusters.

Around the pool area, the hummingbirds can partake of the orange, blue, and white flowers of bird-of-paradise; purple-and-white lantana; yellowish green agave; and the white flowers of yucca, orange, lemon, and jasmine.

On the patio, potted plants for the hummingbirds include blue lobelia; white and pink petunias; as well as geraniums, begonias, impatiens, and snapdragons in colors of orange, red, pink, purple, white, and blue.

My songbirds generally use the flowerbeds, bushes, and trees around the yard for perching on the way to my birdfeeding areas on the open lawn. Although the Scrub Jays use the palm, flowering plum, juniper, and coral trees for a lofty view of the surroundings, they often dive into the oleander to store peanuts and to move about to other areas of the yard or beyond.

The House Finches often perch on the oleander, apricot, and coreopsis, while the Rufous-sided and California Towhees often hop through the understory of the oleander and the flowerbeds and then hop out onto the open lawn from a good vantage point.

The finches eat seeds from the flowerheads of

sweet alyssum, both in the flowerbeds and in pots on the patio. They also eat seed from grasses that I allow to grow in the flowerbeds, and they really enjoy pecking into the apricots when they ripen on the tree in mid-June.

These apricots are at least partially responsible for attracting the male and female Hooded Orioles to the garden. After watching the orioles make repeated visits throughout the day to the apricots, pecking away and drawing the flesh from the fruit, I ran down to my local garden center and purchased an oriole feeder, which I filled with sugar water and hung from a bare stem of the lemon tree by the pool, overlooking the canyon.

Almost immediately, the orioles discovered the feeder, and they have been regular visitors to that lemon tree during the spring and summer. They enjoy the relative safety of their canyon access to the feeder, although sometimes they fly right over the house, patio, and pool to the feeder.

I enjoy watching them through the binoculars as they feed, and I think it is funny the way the feeder swings back and forth after they push off from it and take to the air. I miss them when they fly back to Mexico in the fall.

• • •

THE SURROUNDING
ENVIRONMENT

Your backyard bird garden, of course, does not exist in isolation from the surrounding environment. In my case, my yard borders on a chaparral canyon on the back side of the property, and a suburban street on the front side.

The canyon features scrubland and trees such as the California sycamore and coast live oak, which provide nesting holes and acorns respectively for the Acorn Woodpecker. My Scrub Jays no doubt fly into the canyon from time to time and eat a few acorns themselves.

I occasionally receive avian visitors from the canyon. For instance, every now and then a covey of California Quail walk around the pool and into the brush. This usually occurs at sunrise, and the golden, early-morning sunlight reflecting off the black-and-white head, black plume, and white-striped chestnut sides of the male of this species is a sight to behold.

I also receive occasional visits from the Blue-gray Gnatcatcher, which flits about among the bushes and trees on the back hill, searching for insects and calling out with his distinctive *buzz-buzz, buzz-buzz* call.

My Scrub Jays often fly around the back of the

house and into the tall pine tree at the top of the hill, and then they fly off to an even bigger pine tree on the property next to mine. I hear a lot of screeching from up there, so they must be roosting and nesting in that tree.

Thus, you can include in your garden birds that do not use your mixed birdseed every day—and you can count the various plants and habitats that adjoin your property as part of a garden-at-large that includes all of your neighbors' backyard bird gardens as well as your own.

After all, when a Northern Cardinal, Evening Grosbeak, Scrub Jay, or House Finch flies overhead and sees your plants and birdfeeders, the bird does not distinguish a property line. He sees your yard as part of an overall environment that he is using.

Perhaps the birds' presence in our yards is more of a gift than we realize.

POPULAR PLANTINGS FOR BIRDS

The following plants are some of the most popular for attracting birds to your garden.

TREES

Birch (Betula)—Deciduous, with seeds and flower buds. Attracts chickadees, finches, towhees, woodpeckers, jays, juncos, and titmice. Provide plenty of moisture.

Cherry (Prunus)—Deciduous and evergreen, with fruit. Attracts jays, waxwings, grosbeaks, finches, mockingbirds, robins, sparrows, thrushes, woodpeckers, bluebirds, thrashers, cardinals, and thrushes. Prefers moist, well-drained soil and full sun.

Crabapple (Malus)—Deciduous, with fruit. Attracts mockingbirds, robins, waxwings, grosbeaks, bluebirds, catbirds, finches, flickers, and vireos. Prefers moist, well-drained soil and full sun.

Hawthorn (Crataegus)—Deciduous, with fruit. Attracts grosbeaks, jays, mockingbirds, robins, flickers, finches, sparrows, thrushes, and waxwings. Prefers well-drained soil and full sun or partial shade.

Holly (Ilex)—Evergreen and deciduous, with fruit. Attracts waxwings, robins, bluebirds, jays, thrashers, cardinals, catbirds, flickers, and mockingbirds. Prefers moist, well-drained soil and full sun or partial shade.

Juniper (Juniperus)—Evergreen, with fruit. Attracts grosbeaks, robins, cardinals, waxwings, flickers, mockingbirds, finches, and warblers. Tolerates most soils and prefers full sun or partial shade.

Maple (Acer)—Deciduous, with seeds. Attracts finches, grosbeaks, cardinals, robins, warblers, and waxwings. Prefers plenty of moisture in well-drained soil with full sun or partial shade.

Mulberry (Morus)—Deciduous, with fruit. Attracts finches, grosbeaks, mockingbirds, robins, thrashers, jays, catbirds, waxwings, flickers, orioles, titmice, and vireos. Tolerates most soils and prefers plenty of moisture and full sun.

Oak (Quercus)—Deciduous and evergreen, with acorns. Attracts grosbeaks, jays, nuthatches, titmice, woodpeckers, cardinals, and towhees. Prefers moist, well-drained soil and full sun.

Pine (Pinus)—Evergreen, with seeds. Attracts chickadees, jays, juncos, nuthatches, warblers, woodpeckers, finches, towhees, and grosbeaks. Prefers well-drained soil and full sun.

SHRUBS

Bayberry (Myrica)—Deciduous, with fruit. Attracts finches, chickadees, flickers, robins, thrashers, thrushes, towhees, jays, titmice, catbirds, bluebirds, warblers, and vireos. Prefers moist, well-drained soil in full sun or partial shade.

Blueberry (Vaccinium)—Deciduous and evergreen, with fruit. Attracts bluebirds, flickers, thrashers, thrushes, orioles, titmice, chickadees, towhees, robins, mockingbirds, and catbirds. Prefers an acid, moist soil and full sun or partial shade.

Bramble (Rubus)—Deciduous, with fruit. Attracts cardinals, grosbeaks, robins, sparrows, thrashers, catbirds, flickers, mockingbirds, orioles, quail, thrushes, warblers, waxwings, woodpeckers, and jays. Prefers moist soil and full sun.

Cotoneaster (Cotoneaster)—Evergreen and deciduous, with fruit. Attracts waxwings, mockingbirds, robins, sparrows, bluebirds, thrushes, thrashers, catbirds, jays, and cardinals. Tolerates most soils and prefers full sun and moderate moisture.

Dogwood (Cornus)—Deciduous, with fruit. Attracts bluebirds, cardinals, catbirds, grosbeaks, robins, woodpeckers, thrashers, waxwings, flickers, thrushes, vireos, sparrows, and tanagers. Prefers moist, well-drained soil and full sun or partial shade.

Elderberry (Sambucus)—Deciduous, with fruit. Attracts grosbeaks, flickers, waxwings, jays, mockingbirds, robins, cardinals, catbirds, titmice, nuthatches, finches, bluebirds, woodpeckers, and towhees. Prefers moist, well-drained soil and full sun.

Firethorn (Pyracantha)—Evergreen, with fruit. Attracts finches, cardinals, catbirds, robins, sparrows, thrashers, waxwings, mockingbirds, thrushes, bluebirds, jays, and wrens. Tolerates most soils and prefers moderate moisture and full sun.

Rose (Rosa)—Deciduous, with fruit. Attracts cardinals, waxwings, grosbeaks, mockingbirds, thrushes, bobwhites, thrashers, goldfinches, and robins. Prefers well-drained soil and full sun.

Serviceberry (Amelanchier)—Deciduous, with fruit. Attracts bluebirds, waxwings, grosbeaks, robins, cardinals, catbirds, flickers, thrushes, and finches. Prefers well-drained soil and full sun or partial shade.

Viburnum (Viburnum)—Deciduous and evergreen, with fruit. Attracts cardinals, thrushes, waxwings, bluebirds, grosbeaks, catbirds, flickers, mockingbirds, robins, thrashers, finches, sparrows, and towhees. Prefers moist, well-drained soil and full sun or partial shade.

VINES AND GROUND COVER

Bearberry (Arctostaphylos uva-ursi)—Evergreen ground cover, with fruit. Attracts sparrows, chickadees, mockingbirds, jays, wrens, towhees, thrashers, and thrushes. Prefers well-drained soil and full sun.

Grape (Vitis)—Deciduous vine, with fruit. Attracts jays, cardinals, towhees, robins, bluebirds, finches, mockingbirds, thrashers, thrushes, vireos, catbirds, woodpeckers, orioles, warblers, and waxwings.

Prefers moist, well-drained soil and full sun or partial shade.

Strawberry (Fragaria)—Evergreen ground cover, with fruit. Attracts grosbeaks, towhees, catbirds, mockingbirds, robins, blackbirds, thrashers, thrushes, waxwings, and flickers. Prefers well-drained soil and full sun or partial shade.

Virginia Creeper (Parthenocissus quinquefolia)— Deciduous vine, with fruit. Attracts bluebirds, chickadees, mockingbirds, robins, flickers, titmice, catbirds, thrashers, thrushes, and woodpeckers. Prefers moist, well-drained soil in full sun or shade.

FLOWERS FOR SEED

The following flowers provide seeds for a variety of birds, including finches, goldfinches, cardinals, sparrows, chickadees, nuthatches, towhees, titmice, and doves.

Aster (Aster)—Perennial. Blooms from spring to fall in white, blue, red, and purple. Tolerates most soils and prefers full sun.

Columbine (Aquilegia)—Perennial. Blooms from spring to early summer in various colors. Tolerates most soils and prefers full sun or partial shade.

Coreopsis (Coreopsis)—Annual and perennial.

Blooms from late spring to fall in yellow, orange, and red. Prefers moderate moisture and full sun.

Cornflower (Centaurea cyanus)—Annual. Blooms in summer in blue, pink, rose, red, and white. Prefers moderate moisture and full sun.

Cosmos (Cosmos)—Annual. Blooms from summer to fall in white, pink, rose, purple, yellow, and lavender. Prefers moderate moisture and full sun.

Gloriosa Daisy (Rudbeckia hirta)—Biennial or short-lived perennial, can be grown as an annual. Blooms from summer to fall in yellow, orange, or russet. Tolerates most soils and prefers full sun or partial shade.

Goldenrod (Solidago)—Perennial. Blooms from summer to fall in yellow. Prefers moderate moisture and full sun or partial shade.

Purple Coneflower (Echinacea purpurea)—Perennial. Blooms in late summer in purple. Prefers moderate moisture and full sun.

Sunflower (Helianthus)—Annual and perennial. Blooms in late summer to fall in yellow, orange, and red-brown. Prefers moist, well-drained soil and full sun.

Zinnia (Zinnia)—Annual. Blooms in summer to early fall in many colors. Prefers moist, well-drained soil and full sun.

Hummingbird Flowers

The following plants provide nectar flowers for hummingbirds.

Bee Balm (Monarda didyma)—Perennial. Blooms from June to September in red. Prefers moist soil and full sun or partial shade.

Bottlebrush (Callistemon)—Evergreen shrub or tree. Blooms most of the year, in red. Prefers regular or moderate moisture and full sun.

Cardinal Flower (Lobelia cardinalis)—Perennial. Blooms from May to December in red. Prefers moist soil and full sun or partial shade.

Coralbells (Heuchera sanguinea)—Perennial. Blooms from February to October in red. Prefers moist, well-drained soil and full sun or partial shade.

Fuchsia (Fuchsia)—Evergreen or deciduous shrub. Blooms from early summer to frost in pink, purple, and red, sometimes with white. Prefers moist soil and partial shade.

Honeysuckle (Lonicera)—Evergreen and deciduous shrub or vine. Blooms from spring to frost in white, red, yellow, purple, and pink. Prefers moderate moisture and full sun or partial shade.

Penstemon (Penstemon)—Perennial and evergreen

shrub. Blooms from spring to summer, sometimes longer, in various colors. Prefers regular or moderate moisture and full sun or partial shade.

Phlox *(Phlox)*—Annual and perennial. Blooms from spring to frost in various colors. Prefers moist, well-drained soil and full sun or partial shade.

Sage *(Salvia)*—Annual, biennial, perennial, and shrub. Blooms from spring to frost in various colors. Prefers moist, well-drained soil and full sun or partial shade.

Trumpet Creeper *(Campsis radicans)*—Deciduous vine. Blooms from July to September in orange-red. Prefers regular or moderate moisture and full sun or partial shade.

Water

BIRDBATHS

LIKE US, BIRDS need to drink water to survive. Therefore, providing a good source of water for your birds to drink (as well as for bathing) will go a long way toward attracting as many birds as possible to your garden.

Whether you use a pedestal birdbath, hanging birdbath, or a birdbath placed directly on the ground (or even dug into the soil), your birds will appreciate any effort you make to provide water for them.

In addition to common garden birds such as the Black-capped Chickadee, Evening Grosbeak, Tufted Titmouse,

Northern Mockingbird, and House Sparrow, a bird-bath will attract insect eaters such as the Yellow Warbler and Black Phoebe, as well as birds that usually remain in the bushes, such as the Red-eyed Vireo and the Hermit and Varied Thrushes.

Other birds that often use birdbaths for drinking and bathing include the Cedar Waxwing, American Goldfinch, Song Sparrow, House Finch, Northern Cardinal, American Robin, and Indigo and Painted Buntings.

OTHER WATER SOURCES

Commercially available birdbaths feature materials such as ceramic, concrete, and plastic. However, in addition to commercial birdbaths, you can provide water for your birds in a number of other ways, including filling depressions in large rocks and tree stumps with water. You can also turn a clean garbage can lid upside down on the ground and fill it with water.

In my yard, the Scrub Jays, House Finches, and California Towhees use the cement pedestal bird-bath for drinking and for bathing. However, an equally popular source of drinking water (especially for the towhees) is the ceramic dishes in which the potted plants on the patio around the pool are placed. After I water these potted plants, the towhees invariably hop over to these dishes, dip their beaks into the water by the side of the pots, then tilt their heads back to swallow—repeating this series of actions over and over until they are satiated. On hot summer days, this can take five to ten sips per visit, of which there are a good number throughout the day.

The California Towhees, Scrub Jays, House Finches, and Mourning Doves also sip water regularly from the patio area around the pool, when puddles form after the plants in the yard around the pool are watered.

One day in late August, I saw a female Mourning Dove sitting in a puddle on the patio under the lemon tree and by the jade plant, so the water (along with the bird) was shaded from the hot afternoon sun.

I watched this dove for about ten minutes, as she preened her wing feathers a few times and shifted about in the water, presumably to cool and bathe herself more thoroughly. Then she slowly raised herself out of the water, which was about three inches deep, took a few sips of the liquid, and calmly walked out of the puddle area and disappeared down the path toward the canyon.

After the dove left, I felt the water with my fingers, and sure enough, it felt pretty cool even though the ambient temperature was about eighty degrees Fahrenheit and the sun felt hot on my skin. I marveled at this dove's ability to use all aspects of her environment to enhance her chances of survival.

I have also seen Mourning Doves, as well as Rock Doves, sipping water from puddles formed in the street when homeowners watered their front yards with sprinklers. One hot, sunny day in May, I turned on the sprinklers in my side yard, and my Scrub Jay proceeded to fly through the mist over and over again—each time landing on either the palm tree, the flowering plum, or the roof of the house.

He seemed to be enjoying himself so much that I decided to run through the mist myself in my shorts and T-shirt. Sure enough, it was extremely refreshing to feel that cool water on such a hot day. Who says we cannot learn something from the animals?

BIRDBATH CLEANING AND MAINTENANCE

It is important to clean your birdbaths regularly, and be sure not to make the water too deep for the birds. Two to three inches is ample, and it is preferable to have a slope toward the edges, where the water should be one-half inch to an inch deep. You can also add some large, flat stones to the bottom of the bird-

bath to provide some perching spots for the birds, and to make the water more shallow.

Provide fresh water for the birds regularly. This may require refilling your birdbaths at least once each day during hot weather, as birds are reluctant to drink from stale, warm water, especially if it is also dirty. However, the reward of seeing your finches, chickadees, cardinals, and jays descending to drink and bathe is incentive enough to keep a cool, clean water supply in your birdbaths. In addition, if you provide a reliable source of water, birds will know that they can depend on your yard for drinking and bathing, as well as for food, and this will make them all the more loyal to your yard.

RUNNING WATER

Birds love the sound of running or dripping water, and resourceful backyard bird gardeners have devised a number of systems over the years for delivering moving water to the birds.

At its simplest, a bucket with a tiny hole in it can

be placed over your birdbath, resulting in a slow, steady drip that only requires one refilling of the bucket each day.

You can also suspend a garden hose over your birdbath and turn on the water just a tiny bit to supply the dripping that you desire.

Some commercially available birdbaths feature electric pumps that recirculate the water to a high spot from which the water cascades down a series of waterfalls. Others feature built-in drippers and misters, the former of which attracts birds year-round while the latter is particularly attractive to hummingbirds in the summertime.

Some friends of mine in Los Angeles built an elaborate fountain into the wall of their back patio. Water cascades out of three spouts and three two-foot-wide spillways into a pool filled with carp and a series of tall papyrus plants.

The sound of the water is loud, but it doesn't bother a male Anna's Hummingbird that visits the top spillway of this fountain many times throughout the day.

Perching on the metal lip of this spillway, the hummingbird takes occasional sips of water as it flows by and spills over the side all around him. He also sometimes dips his wings and tail feathers into the water as well, then shakes himself off—taking a mini-bath, as it were.

Since a layer of algae has formed on the bottom of the spillway, the hummingbird is no doubt being treated to extra nutrients in this water—and he surely catches insects either in the water or flying by him at his perch.

The fountain was not built for this hummingbird—but you could not tell *him*.

POOLS

Some backyard bird gardeners build a pool right into the ground. This can be accomplished in a number of ways. One simple technique involves burying a container such as a birdbath bowl. Simply dig a hole in the shape of the bowl, place the bowl in the depression, and fill the edges in with dirt. Be sure to position the bowl about 2 inches above the surrounding area, to be sure that dirt and other matter does not wash into the pool.

A more elaborate pool-building technique involves digging a shallow hole, covering the soil with a flexible rubber or plastic liner, then placing small stones or gravel on the bottom of the pool and large rocks around the perimeter. A recirculating pump can be built into such a pool, and one commercially available model even features a small waterfall.

If you place ferns, grasses, and aquatic plants such as water lily both in and around your pool, you can create a waterside environment that will not only attract common backyard birds such as robins, jays, and chickadees, but also such birds as swallows, Purple Martins, and phoebes, which nest near water.

PLACEMENT OF BIRDBATHS AND POOLS

Be sure to place your birdbaths and pools in an open area, with plenty of good perching opportunities nearby for the birds. This way, the birds will have a clear view of the water, and they will also have a number of escape routes if they sense danger. (Some birds, such as thrushes, warblers, and towhees, prefer to drink and bathe either adjacent to or among bushes or in a wooded area. If you place a birdbath

near a shrubby area, be sure that the birdbath is at least three feet high, so as to protect your drinking and bathing birds from predators such as cats that may be lurking in the shrubbery.)

Remember, also, to place your birdbaths and pools where they can easily be viewed from inside your house. This way, you will be helping the birds and entertaining yourself at the same time.

After all, this is what a backyard bird garden is all about!

BIRDBATHS IN WINTER

Although all birds require water year-round for drinking and bathing, it is particularly important to provide your birds with a fresh source of water during the winter, when they need your help the most.

For one thing, obtaining water from snow or ice requires a great deal of energy on the bird's part to thaw its frozen treat. Therefore, if you provide your birds with a reliable supply of drinking water in your birdbaths or pools, you will be saving your precious friends a significant amount of the energy that they need in order to survive during the winter months.

Furthermore, since birds require regular baths even in winter to keep their feathers clean for maximum insulation and flight capabilities, backyard bird gardeners may actually see more birds bathing at their birdbaths during the winter than during the warmer times of the year.

To keep the water in your birdbaths and small pools from freezing during the winter, you can periodically add hot water, as needed. This will certainly keep you busy.

Or you can purchase an electrical immersion heater. Since immersion heaters are equipped with thermostats, they will keep the water from freezing, but will shut off when the water's temperature reaches forty degrees Fahrenheit or so. Some commercially available birdbaths are even equipped with built-in heaters and thermostats.

CHAPTER

SIX

Birdhouses

PLACING A NUMBER of birdhouses in your backyard bird garden will attract a wide variety of cavity-nesting birds to your yard.

Depending on which bird species reside in your area, and which habitats they prefer, you may enjoy watching everything from small birds such as the Black-capped Chickadee, Tufted Titmouse, and Red-breasted Nuthatch to larger birds such as the Barred Owl, American Kestral, and Northern Flicker raise their families from year to year.

BIRDHOUSE DIMENSIONS

Whether your birdhouses are purchased commercially or made from scratch, their dimensions must conform to the requirements of each species you wish to attract, and the birdhouses must be placed in the habitat that the birds naturally use for nesting.

For instance, the Black-capped Chickadee uses an entrance hole 1⅛ inches in diameter, and its birdhouse should be placed in an area that has plenty of trees. The Eastern, Western, and Mountain Blue-

birds, on the other hand, use entrance holes 1½ inches in diameter, and their birdhouses should be placed in open areas such as fields and farmlands.

The Northern Flicker uses an entrance hole 2½ inches in diameter, and it utilizes both open and wooded habitats for nesting. The Wood Duck uses an entrance hole four inches in diameter and prefers a wooded area either near or above a body of water for nesting.

NESTING MATERIALS

It is a good idea to leave some nesting materials such as grasses, twigs, bark, hair, feathers, cloth, and string for your birdhouse birds, as well as for your open nesters. These materials can be placed in empty suet baskets or mesh bags that are hung from trees, or they can be placed in an open area on the ground. Be sure that any pieces of cloth or string are no longer than four to six inches in length, so that your birds will not become entangled in them.

WHERE TO PLACE BIRDHOUSES

Birdhouses should be mounted on sturdy poles, or they can be attached to trees or the walls of buildings. To protect the birds from the elements, your birdhouses should face away from the direction of the prevailing winds in your area. Birdhouses should also be tilted slightly forward, so that rain will not fall into the entrance hole.

Hanging birdhouses are acceptable for wrens, which have been known to build nests in everything from clothes hanging on a clothesline to mailboxes, tin cans, hats, boots, and shoes. Wrens will also build nests inside hanging gourds, as will Purple Martins.

• • •

PURPLE MARTINS

The Purple Martin causes quite a stir when it returns each spring to various sections of North America from its wintering grounds in South America.

Since Purple Martins nest in colonies of up to three hundred birds, special Purple Martin houses can either be purchased commercially or made from scratch to accommodate eight or sixteen pairs at first, with more compartments to be added later, as you desire.

Purple Martin "hotels" should be placed in a wide-open area, preferably near water, where the

insects on which the Purple Martins feed will be breeding.

BLUEBIRDS

The Eastern, Western, and Mountain Bluebirds are also the recipients of customized housing arrangements, courtesy of backyard bird gardeners across North America.

Because much of the bluebird's open habitat has been destroyed since early in this century, and because the introduced House Sparrow and European Starling have successfully competed for natural bluebird nesting sites, the bluebird has seen its numbers fall drastically until recent years, when conservation efforts on the bird's behalf have led to a resurgence of its numbers.

Bluebird houses can be purchased commercially, or you can make them yourself. They consist of a 1½-inch-diameter entrance hole, with a five-by-five-inch floor area, and should be mounted on a pole or fence post about three to six feet high. The entrance hole is too small for the European Starling, and the floor plan is too small for the House Sparrow—and the birdhouse is placed too low for the latter species as well.

Bluebird houses are often positioned in a long line, or trail, throughout the countryside. Because bluebirds are territorial, your bluebird houses should

Birdhouse Dimensions

Bird	Floor Area (in.)	Height (in.)	Hole Diam. (in.)	Height of Hole Above Floor (in.)	Height of House Above Ground (ft.)	Location
Bluebird	5×5	8–12	1½	6–10	3–6	Open fields and meadows
Chickadee	4×4	8–12	1⅛	6–8	4–15	Wooded areas, forest edges
Flycatchers (Ash-throated, Great-crested)	6×6	8–12	1½–2½	6–10	5–20	Open areas, woods
House Finch	6×6	6–12	1⅜–2½	4–7	5–20	Backyards, trees, shrubs
Northern Flicker	7×7	14–24	2½	10–20	6–30	Open areas, woods, farmlands
Nuthatches (Red-breasted, White-breasted)	4×4	8–12	1⅛–1½	6–8	5–25	Wooded areas, forest edges
Prothonotary Warbler	4×4	6–12	1⅛–1½	4–7	4–12	Wooded swamps
Purple Martin	6×6	6	2–2½	1–2¼	6–25	Open areas, near water
Swallows (Tree, Violet-green)	5×5	6–12	1½	1–7	5–15	Open areas, near water
Titmouse	4×4	8–12	1–1½	6–10	4–15	Wooded areas, forest edges
Wood Duck	12×12	22–25	4	16–18	5–20	Wooded swamps
Woodpecker (Downy)	4×4	8–14	1¼–1½	6–12	5–25	Wooded areas, forest edges
Woodpeckers (Hairy, Red-bellied, Red-headed)	6×6	12–16	2	6–14	8–20	Wooded areas, forest edges
Wrens (Bewick's, House, Carolina)	4×4	6–12	1–1½	4–7	4–10	Wooded areas, forest edges

be placed anywhere from two hundred to four hundred feet apart. A tree, shrub, or pole should be anywhere from five to a hundred feet away as a convenient perch so the fledglings will have a safe place to rest after they fly out of the birdhouse for the first time.

NESTING SHELVES

The American Robin, Eastern and Black Phoebes, and Barn Swallow build nests on the ledges of houses, barns, garages, and other structures.

They can be enticed to your buildings if you construct wooden nesting shelves and place these shelves under the eaves of a building. Since these species need mud to build their nests, you should keep a shallow container of mud in your yard or perhaps have an area of wet soil—preferably with some clay in it to make it sticky.

Nesting Shelf Dimensions

Bird	Floor Area (in.)	Height (in.)	Height of Shelf Above Ground (ft.)	Location
American Robin	6×8	8	6–15	On buildings
Barn Swallow	6×6	6	8–12	On buildings
Phoebe	6×6	6	8–12	On buildings

PROTECTING YOUR BIRDHOUSES

You can protect your birdhouses (and the treasures inside them!) in a number of ways from predators such as raccoons, squirrels, snakes, and cats.

If your birdhouse is mounted on a post or pole, you can place a cone-shaped squirrel baffle (such as the one used for your pole-mounted birdfeeders) on the pole beneath the birdhouse. Backyard bird gardeners also place grease on these metal poles or wrap wooden posts with sheet-metal strips about two feet in height to deter predators.

Metal strips can also be wrapped around trees that contain birdhouses, but be sure that the strip is attached loosely, so the tree can breathe and grow.

BIRDHOUSE CLEANING AND MAINTENANCE

Birdhouses should be cleaned after each brood. Remove the old nest and thoroughly brush out the interior of the birdhouse. Then scrub the birdhouse with water and allow it to dry.

During the winter, cover the entrance holes of your birdhouses to discourage pests such as mice and squirrels from nesting in them—or bring the birdhouses inside until the spring.

Then, you will be treated to the whole dance again, as birds such as the Downy, Hairy, and Red-bellied Woodpeckers; Eastern and Western Screech Owls; Tree and Violet-green Swallows; and Prothonotary Warbler arrive to start their families for another year.

Twenty Common Garden Birds

THIS CHAPTER LISTS twenty species of birds that commonly occur in the continental United States and Canada. Depending on the region in which you live, you may attract any of these birds to your garden.

MOURNING DOVE
(Zenaida macroura)

Description—12" long. Gray-brown plumage with long, pointed tail that has white tips on the feathers. Males and females look alike.

Range—Throughout U.S. and southern Canada.

Natural Food—Seeds and insects.

Food for Attracting—Mixed birdseed, especially millet and cracked corn.

Special Features—Wings make a whistling sound when the bird takes flight.

DOWNY WOODPECKER
(Picoides pubescens)

Description—6¾" long. Black-and-white above, white below, with a short bill. Males have a red patch on the nape.

Range—Most of U.S. and Canada, except parts of southern Arizona, New Mexico, and Texas.

Natural Food—Insects; also fruits and seeds.

Food for Attracting—Suet, sunflower seeds, peanut-butter mixtures.

Special Features—Smallest North American woodpecker, and the most common North American woodpecker in backyards.

BLUE JAY
(Cyanocitta cristata)

Description—11" long. Bright blue above, white

below, with black necklace. Also features a prominent crest. Males and females look alike.

Range—Eastern U.S. and southern Canada, east of the Rocky Mountains.

Natural Food—Seeds, nuts (especially acorns), fruits, insects.

Food for Attracting—Mixed birdseed (especially sunflower seeds), peanuts, suet, cracked corn, bread.

Special Features—Similar species in the West include the Scrub Jay *(Aphelocoma coerulescens)*, which also occurs in Florida, and the Steller's Jay *(Cyanocitta stelleri)*.

BLACK-CAPPED CHICKADEE
(Parus atricapillus)

Description—5¼″ long. Black cap and throat, white cheeks, gray above, white below, and buff flanks. Males and females look alike.

Range—Northern half of U.S.; Alaska, Canada.

Natural Food—Insects, seeds, fruits.

Food for Attracting—Sunflower seeds, peanuts, suet, baked goods.

Special Features—Black-capped Chickadees often appear in flocks and are very active as they flit about in your garden.

TUFTED TITMOUSE
(Parus bicolor)

Description—6″ long. Gray above, white below, with buff flanks and a gray crest (black in Texas). Males and females look alike.

Range—Most of eastern U.S.

Natural Food—Insects, seeds, fruits.

Food for Attracting—Sunflower seeds, peanuts, suet, baked goods.

Special Features—Plain Titmouse *(Parus inornatus)* is a similar species in the West.

WHITE-BREASTED NUTHATCH
(Sitta carolinensis)

Description—5¾″ long. Blue-gray above and white below; males have a black cap and females have a gray cap.

Range—Most of U.S. and southern Canada; absent in much of the Great Plains area.

Natural Food—Nuts, seeds, insects, fruits.

Food for Attracting—Sunflower seeds, peanuts, suet, baked goods.

Special Features—Red-breasted Nuthatch *(Sitta canadensis)* is a similar species that is common throughout most of North America.

HOUSE WREN
(Troglodytes aedon)

Description—4¾" long. Dark brown above, lighter brown below, with a short, often upturned tail. Males and females look alike.

Range—Throughout U.S. and southern Canada.

Natural Food—Insects and spiders.

Food for Attracting—Suet, bread.

Special Features—Will nest in such disparate places as pockets of clothes hanging on clotheslines, boots, hats, mailboxes, flowerpots, and watering cans.

AMERICAN ROBIN
(Turdus migratorius)

Description—10" long. Dark gray above, red-breasted, with a black head and tail in males and a gray head and tail in females.

Range—Throughout U.S. and Canada.

Natural Food—Earthworms, insects, fruit.

Food for Attracting—Suet, peanut-butter mixtures, fruit, bread.

Special Features—The American Robin is a traditional harbinger of spring in northern areas, and fortunate bird gardeners may catch a glimpse of its beautiful blue eggs.

NORTHERN MOCKINGBIRD
(Mimus polyglottos)

Description—10″ long. Gray above, paler below, with white patches on the wings and tail that are conspicuous in flight. Males and females look alike.

Range—U.S. and southern Canada, except Northwest.

Natural Food—Insects, fruit, seeds.

Food for Attracting—Fruit (especially raisins), suet, peanut-butter mixtures, baked goods.

Special Features—The Northern Mockingbird's song can go on for hours, and it mimics many of your neighborhood birds'.

EUROPEAN STARLING
(Sturnus vulgaris)

Description—8″ long. In spring, iridescent black with a yellow bill; in fall and winter, speckled with a dark bill. Males and females look alike.

Range—Throughout U.S. and Canada.

Natural Food—Insects, earthworms, seeds, fruit.

Food for Attracting—Cracked corn, peanuts, fruit, suet, baked goods.

Special Features—Introduced to North America from Europe in 1890, this species often congregates in large flocks and has displaced many native cavity nesters, such as bluebirds.

NORTHERN CARDINAL
(Cardinalis cardinalis)

Description—8¾″ long. Males are red, with a prominent crest, black face, and red bill. Females are buff-brown with a red-tinged crest, wings, and tail, and a red bill.

Range—Eastern U.S. from Great Plains to southern Ontario, Quebec, and Nova Scotia; also in Texas and parts of the Southwest.

Natural Food—Seeds, fruits, and insects.

Food for Attracting—Sunflower seeds, cracked corn, peanuts.

Special Features—One of the few birds that sing year-round, the Northern Cardinal also offers an unforgettable vision when seen against a snowy, white background.

SONG SPARROW
(Melospiza melodia)

Description—6¼″ long. Brown above, white and heavily streaked below with a large, central breast spot. Males and females look alike.

Range—Throughout U.S. and Canada.

Natural Food—Insects, seeds, fruit.

Food for Attracting—Mixed birdseed (especially sunflower seeds), peanuts, bread.

Special Features—Aptly named, the Song Sparrow has a wildly variable song that can be heard at all times of the year.

DARK-EYED JUNCO
(Junco hyemalis)

Description—6¼" long. Variable. Mostly eastern "Slate-colored" form is gray above, white below; Great Basin and southern Rocky Mountain "Gray-headed" form is similar, but has a brown back; mostly western "Oregon" form is similar, but has a black head; and the "White-winged" form is similar, but has two white wing bars. Females are generally duller than males.

Range—Throughout U.S. and Canada.

Natural Food—Seeds, insects, fruit.

Food for Attracting—Sunflower seeds, millet, cracked corn, peanuts, bread.

Special Features—Called the snowbird, the Dark-eyed Junco is often seen in backyards after a snowstorm as it digs through the snow for seeds that have been buried.

RED-WINGED BLACKBIRD
(Agelaius phoeniceus)

Description—8¾" long. Males are black with red shoulders; females are brown above, streaked below.

Range—Throughout U.S. and Canada.

Natural Food—Seeds, insects.

Food for Attracting—Cracked corn, mixed birdseed, peanuts, bread.

Special Features—In recent years, because of access to food from backyard birdfeeders, more and more Red-winged Blackbirds have been remaining in the North during the winter, instead of migrating to the South.

BROWN-HEADED COWBIRD
(Molothrus ater)

Description—7½" long. Males are black with a brown head; females are grayish brown.

Range—Throughout U.S. and Canada.

Natural Food—Insects, seeds, fruit.

Food for Attracting—Cracked corn, mixed birdseed, peanuts, bread.

Special Features—Females lay their eggs in the nests of other birds, which rear the cowbird young at the expense of their own.

HOUSE FINCH
(Carpodacus mexicanus)

Description—6″ long. Males are brown above, streaked below, with a red (sometimes orange or yellow) forehead, breast, and rump; females are brown above and streaked below.

Range—Throughout most of U.S., except some central areas; southeastern and southwestern Canada.

Natural Food—Seeds, fruit, insects.

Food for Attracting—Mixed birdseed (especially sunflower seeds), thistle, peanuts, suet, bread.

Special Features—House Finches often feed in groups, singing their delightful *cheweep* call to each other.

PINE SISKIN
(Carduelis pinus)

Description—5″ long. Brown above, streaked below, with patches of yellow on the wings and tail. Males and females look alike.

Range—Throughout U.S. and Canada.

Natural Food—Seeds, insects.

Food for Attracting—Thistle, sunflower seeds, peanuts, suet.

I N D E X

Index

Index